CW01064175

BLACKPOLE
MUNITIONS FACTORY

BLACKPOLE MUNITIONS FACTORY

by
Colin Jones

Logaston Press

LOGASTON PRESS
Little Logaston Woonton Almeley
Herefordshire HR3 6QH
logastonpress.co.uk

First published by Logaston Press 2017
Copyright text © Colin Jones and Mick Wilks
Copyright illustrations © as per credits and acknowledgements

All rights reserved. No part of this publication
may be reproduced, stored in a retrieval system,
or transmitted, in any form or by any means,
electronic, mechanical, photocopying, recording
or otherwise, without the prior permission,
in writing, of the publisher

ISBN 978 1 910839 13 3

Typeset by Logaston Press
and printed and bound in Poland by
www.lfbookservices.co.uk

CONTENTS

The author, the late Colin Jones, provides scale for one of three surviving open-topped pillboxes that formed part of a circle of defences around the Blackpole factory from 1940 onwards, this one located at Spellis Green. Blackpole had been designated as a Vulnerable Point by the Home Guard and was to be defended against air or ground attack should Britain have been invaded by German forces in the Second World War. (Photo by Mick Wilks, 1990s)

ACKNOWLEDGEMENTS

I am aware from his working files that Colin had been helped by a number of people and organisations to assemble the information and illustrations about the Blackpole factory that make up this account.

Firstly, I know that he would want to thank Malcolm Atkin, the former County Archaeology Officer, and his staff, for the practical help and encouragement they have given to all of the volunteer researchers who worked on the original Defence of Britain Project, and the follow-up Defence of Worcestershire Project. Malcolm's successor, Victoria Bryant, now head of the combined Worcestershire Archive and Archaeology Service (WAAS) at The Hive in Worcester, and her staff in both arms of the service, continue to support the project. In particular Colin would wish to thank the Historic Environment Section for their continuing help, and the staff, notably Dr Adrian Gregson, of the Archive Section for bringing to his attention a most important collection of papers and photographs relating to the Blackpole factory held in the archive. Further afield he would wish to thank the staff at the National Archive at Kew for their help – a list of the numerous files he consulted there is included in the sources of information at the end of this account. The Cadbury Archive at Bournville was especially helpful to him and he would want me to thank, in particular, Sarah Foden, Information Manager/Archivist of Cadbury Archive, Mondelez International, who facilitated his research there. In addition the Imperial War Museum has contributed the image on page 45, and the Mercian Regiment Museum, Worcester, has provided that on page 36.

The *Worcester News* organisation, notably the editor, Peter John, and Mike Pryce, have provided both information and illustrations for this publication, which are gratefully acknowledged. In fact Colin's research was given an initial boost by the *Worcester News* of 24 June 2009 which published a letter setting out his intentions and seeking contact with former employees at the factory, or who had lived at the associated workers' hostel, or could provide information and photographs. Consequently Colin was contacted by a number of people who had worked at the factory, or had had family members who had worked there during the Second World War, and whose first-hand experiences have made a most important contribution to the research. They are, in alphabetical order: Mrs Mary Addison (née Young), Mrs D. Banner (née Mills), Mrs D. Bowen, Mrs Kathleen Brewer (née Wright), Mrs Ida Cale (née Phillips), Mrs Kathleen Halford (née Telfer, a contact facilitated by the late Ed Hargraves for which Colin was most grateful), Mrs Joan Jacobs (née Turner), Mrs Doris Monk (née Rouse), Ken Murton, Mrs Kathleen Smith (née Driver), Mrs Doreen Stevenson and Mrs Daisy Wide (née Oakley). Latterly, two further people have been in touch to say that relatives had worked at the factory during the Second World War: Valerie Davies whose mother, Peggy Law (née Rann), was there and both have subsequently supplied information and a photograph of Malvern Hall Hostel; and Bryan Massie, whose late mother, Margaret (née McKerron) had also been there. He has correspondence from those days and a number of items and photographs which belonged to his mother. Some of these are illustrated here. Separately, I had interviewed Clifford Lord, former Worcester City Councillor, primarily to contribute to my own study of the Home Guard in Worcestershire, but since he also worked as an apprentice at the Blackpole munitions factory in the Second World War, he was able to throw further light on the activities there. His most valuable testimony has been gratefully added to the account. Other individuals who have contributed are Gill Lawley, Mark Sinclair, and Colin's brother-in-law, Mick Hodgetts who, using his skill with a computer, was able to enhance some of the collected photographs. Andrew Smith, of the Industrial Railway Society, also contributed to Colin's research, specifically about the narrow gauge railway system at Blackpole and by providing a note on his mother's time at the factory in the Second World War. A former colleague of mine and noted railway modeller, John Loynes, has provided detailed information and a photograph of the now rare Flying Banana diesel rail car. I want also to thank my nephew, Paul Turner, for photographing the women's memorial in Whitehall.

Bernard Lowry, the former Regional Coordinator for the Midlands Area of the initial Defence of Britain Project, has been a good friend and mentor to both Colin and me in our role of volunteer researchers of defence sites. I am aware that Bernard looked at some of Colin's initial work on this account, and made a number of very helpful suggestions as to how it might be improved. I recall that Colin was most grateful for this contribution and I acknowledge it here. More recently, both Bernard and Malcolm Atkin have also helped me in explaining some of the detailed characteristics of small arms ammunition referred to in the account and, in Malcolm's case, providing a number of illustrations for the book from his immense collection of wartime ephemera. I also know from our previous dealings with Logaston Press that Colin would have been most grateful to Andy and Karen Johnson for bringing this publication to fruition. Finally, these acknowledgements would not be complete without thanking Colin's wife, Sylvia, for her love and support in all that he did.

Mick Wilks,
December 2016

PREFACE

The initiative for producing a published history of the Blackpole munitions factory was entirely that of the late Colin Jones. Sadly he died before he could complete the task, but much of what you will read on the succeeding pages is the result of his research and writing. I recall that the research had been particularly frustrating for him and, after spending long hours at the National Archive in London, he would often say to me, after he had returned to Worcester, that he had found only very little about the factory, or sometimes nothing at all. Other sources were tapped until he felt he had enough to start writing the story. It seems to me to be a fitting tribute to his hard work for his efforts to be brought to fruition in this publication. With the agreement of his wife, Sylvia, it has been my privilege to help complete the task for my good friend and colleague. Sylvia actually worked at the Blackpole factory in the 1950s and '60s, before leaving to get married, and has provided me with an insight to life at Cadbury's in the post-war era.

As volunteer researchers, Colin and I had been recording modern defence sites in Worcestershire for the County Archaeology Service since 1995, first as a contribution to the national Defence of Britain Project and later, when the national project was wound up in 2002, for the Defence of Worcestershire Project. Over the years a number of other volunteers had made contributions to the study, and now some 2,500 sites of a defence nature have been added to the Worcestershire Historic Environment Record, a database which is held both as a paper record and as a computer file by the Archaeology Service. The database includes many aspects of wartime activity, both military and civil, and spans the 18th, 19th and 20th centuries. The responsibility for entering the results of our combined research into both databases was primarily that of Colin who, being a 'systems man', was happy to tap away at a computer, in addition to carrying out research and site surveying.

Colin and I first visited the Blackpole site in the late 1990s in order to photograph surviving Second World War defence structures around the former munitions factory for the original Defence of Britain Project, the factory complex being recorded at that time in only very general terms. At some stage, Colin decided that he wanted to put more effort into recording the history of the factory and started his quest for information. With the 100th anniversary of First World War events being commemorated, it is timely to expose at least some of the story of the Blackpole munitions factory, which was built in 1916 and began producing small arms ammunition in the following year.

The County Council's Archive and Archaeology Service is one of a number of cultural and heritage organisations from across the county commemorating the 100th anniversary of the First World War with a four-year programme of events and activities under the banner of 'Worcestershire World War One Hundred', supported by a grant from the Heritage Lottery fund. The programme reflects the role that the county played in that conflict and includes recording the stories of Worcestershire people involved and the personal legacy that derives from them. This book makes a contribution to that legacy and has benefited in part from the Heritage Lottery grant mentioned above. For a full programme of events, please visit: http://www.ww1worcestershire.co.uk or follow @ww1worcs.

Coincidentally, the Council for British Archaeology (CBA) has launched a national project entitled 'The Home Front Legacy 1914-1918' to record sites and buildings used in the First World War for wartime purposes and invite volunteers to submit information to the CBA in order to create a national database along the lines of the former Defence of Britain Project (1995-2002). This information will also be added to the Historic Environment Record in each county. For further information on this project and how to become involved, please visit: http://www.homefrontlegacy.org.uk. This book will also provide information for that project.

Mick Wilks,
December 2016

1   INTRODUCTION

It has been said that it took just two bullets to start the First World War – the one which fatally injured Archduke Ferdinand of Austria on 28 June 1914, the other killing his wife – but it was subsequently estimated that another 50,000 bullets were expended for each of the servicemen who died in that conflict.[1] This seems excessive but whether true or not, the quantity of small arms ammunition consumed during that Great War was clearly prodigious and would result in the construction, amongst a number of others, of the munitions factory at Blackpole, on the north side of Worcester. But let us go back a little further in time to consider why this should have been necessary.

The British Army that went to war in 1914 was the product of the reforms introduced in 1908 by the then newly appointed Liberal Secretary of State for War, Richard Burdon Haldane who, like many of his successors, was attempting to cut the costs of providing a peace-time army. His solution was to propose a two-line Army with a regular striking force of three army corps supported by a combination of the former volunteer forces, including the yeomanry, volunteer rifle companies and artillery batteries, to be called the Territorial Force, which would be primarily responsible for home defence. The regular arm of the Army was then largely a colonial police force, with one battalion, or in some cases two, of each regiment serving abroad in various parts of the empire, while the remaining battalions were based in Britain, training new recruits.[2]

The consequence of these reforms was that when Britain declared war on Germany on 4 August 1914, the British Expeditionary Force (BEF) sent to France, although well trained and able to 'punch above its weight', was inadequate both in size and in equipment for the task and would very quickly have to be expanded to fully support the French and Belgian troops fighting on the Western Front. To put the size of that initial BEF in context, it comprised of just four infantry divisions, a cavalry division and one independent brigade which equates to less than 100,000 men. In contrast, Germany's army in 1914 was approximately 800,000 strong, while France could put 820,000, plus 45,000 colonial troops, in the field.[3] However, in compensation, a particular strength of the regular troops of the British Army then was the ability of each trained infantryman using his .303 calibre Short Magazine Lee Enfield rifle to fire 15 aimed rounds per minute. This rate of fire would come as a great shock to the attacking German troops in the opening phases of the Great War, who thought that they were facing machine guns. However, this rate of fire would also use up the 150 rounds carried into battle by each infantryman in about ten minutes. Fire control would clearly become an important issue for riflemen in this war and a cut out device was fitted to the rifles in an effort to control the rate of fire.

Lord Kitchener, the then Secretary of State for War, very quickly realised that the British Army would need rapid expansion in order to contribute more to the allied effort on the Western Front and that this was going to be a long war. Consequently, he made his now famous call for volunteers, the response to which was so great that it allowed, in due time, the creation of three separate armies. However this was to be followed by the introduction of conscription in 1916, after the enthusiasm for volunteering waned. By the end of the Great War, about 5 million men had passed through the ranks of the British Army,[4] and its battlegrounds had expanded beyond the Western Front to include East and West Africa, Salonika (Greece), Gallipoli (Turkey), Palestine (now Israel) and Mesopotamia (now Iraq). As the war progressed, the increasing use of automatic weapons, not only by the infantry, but with the development of aircraft used by the Royal Flying Corps, each carrying two or more automatic weapons, and the introduction of tanks (some versions having up to five machine guns as their armament), would all add substantially to the demand for the standard British small arms ammunition. The annual production figures of machine guns provide a measure of just how the use of automatic weapons used by the British armed services increased in that period:[5]

1914	287
1915	6,102
1916	33,507
1917	79,746
1918	120,864
Total	240,506

The rate of fire and length of some actions on the Western Front with the Vickers machine gun was impressive, it not being unusual for a single gun to fire 60,000 rounds of .303 calibre ammunition in a day. One Australian machine gunner was quoted as saying that his unit had been highly commended for putting down a barrage with 14 guns continually firing for seven hours, with only a few minor stops.[6]

The so-called shell scandal grabbed the newspaper headlines in May 1915, when Sir John French blamed the inadequate supply and quality of artillery shells for having considerably frustrated his ability to fight battles successfully, resulting in a high casualty rate of his troops. In fact the expanding British Army was short of just about everything. The pre-war arrangements for the supply of armaments and ammunition using just a few trusted firms and the Woolwich Arsenal, with the orders being processed through the bureaucratic War Office, proved to be too slow and incapable of supplying sufficient munitions for the purpose. After quickly passing the Munitions of War Act on 9 June 1915, despite resistance from the War Office, the then newly formed coalition government established the Ministry of Munitions on the same day. David Lloyd George, previously the Chancellor of the Exchequer, was appointed Minister of Munitions and gradually brought the ordering and supply of munitions under the control of the new ministry, which set about massively increasing the rate of production. He established a number of management departments at the ministry and put men who he described as having 'push and go', in charge of each section. These managers were largely recruited from private industry.

The definition of 'munitions' in the Act was 'anything required for war purposes and including arms, ammunition, warlike stores or material, and anything required for equipment or transport purposes or for production of munitions'. The resulting increase in production was achieved by constructing new industrial buildings, the ministry consequently becoming a direct employer of industrial labour and, to an even greater extent, bringing under its direct control private firms and their workforce already engaged in munitions' manufacture. The selection of sites for the new factories, design of the works, the manufacture of plant and machinery, together with the recruitment of labour was a complex process, but nevertheless, by the spring of 1916, the first of the new National Factories were producing munitions for Kitchener's volunteer armies in preparation for the Somme offensive starting in July that summer.[7]

Fig. 1.1 Machine guns in all their forms were prodigious users of ammunition, none more so than the British Vickers machine gun illustrated here. After the initial battles of the First World War, and after the Machine Gun Corps had been formed, Vickers guns were used en masse to lay down 'beaten zones', firing over, and very often out of sight of, the attacking British forces to suppress opposition fire, and to prevent the enemy bringing forward reinforcements. It was not unusual for 60,000 rounds to be fired by just one gun during the course of a day's action. The demand for .303 ammunition was consequently enormous and would lead, inter alia, to the construction of the Blackpole Cartridge Factory No. 3 in 1916. The Vickers machine gun remained on the British army's weapons inventory until 1960.

Inevitably, the expansion of British industrial capacity was hampered by Kitchener's call for volunteers for the armed forces. His recruitment drive had resulted in the withdrawal of a substantial proportion of the industrial workforce, including many skilled men who had volunteered for military service in significant numbers. Although some 40,000 of these men would later be released from the services to return to work in industry, it was clear that there was stiff competition between the requirements of the expanding Army and the manpower needs of the munitions' industry. A direct consequence of this was the policy of the Ministry of Munitions of employing semi-skilled and unskilled men and boys, as well as a high proportion of women to tackle the complex industrial activities previously undertaken by the skilled men – a process that became known as 'dilution' and the new workforce as 'dilutees'. Inevitably this would cause difficulties with the trade unions, notably with regard to the restrictive practices which had hitherto prevailed in industry, and would need to be overcome. In addition, excessive drinking of alcohol by the workforce, tolerated beforehand, now interfered with output to an unacceptable degree and would directly lead to the control of drinking hours, a restriction that was only relaxed in the 1990s. Lloyd George took the view that 'drinking was doing more damage in the war than all the German submarines put together'.[8] Another impact of the First World War, which is still with us now, was the bi-annual clock changes to adjust the daylight hours between summer and winter.

It is against this background that the Ministry of Munitions constructed No.3 Cartridge Factory at Blackpole. Its establishment and use during the First World War and its subsequent chequered history is described in the following pages.

Fig. 1.2 Taken from the railway bridge over the Worcester and Birmingham Canal, this panorama of the east side of the Blackpole factory site was taken after the First World War, when Cadbury Brothers were using the site as an outstation for their Bournville chocolate making factory. Prominent in the picture is the chimney for the factory heating boilers, housed in the adjoining building; the stacks of timber used for making chocolate boxes; the wharf in use to the right; the pig sties used for supplementing rations during the First World War; and the clerestorey roof lights of the main factory building peeping over the nearer buildings. (Courtesy of the Cadbury Archive, Mondelez International)

2   BLACKPOLE AND THE FIRST WORLD WAR

Building the Blackpole factory

At the start of the 20th century, in addition to the Royal Arsenal at Woolwich the War Office had been reliant on a number of non-ferrous metal manufacturers to provide its small arms ammunition requirements. In the Birmingham area, these were the Birmingham Metal and Munitions Company, the Kings Norton Metal Company and Ely Brothers & Kynock. The increase in production capacity for both small arms and the ammunition to go with them, precipitated by the expansion of the British and Commonwealth armed forces, and the increasing use of automatic weapons, was provided for by an expansion of both the existing trade and the creation of the government's own industrial capacity by the provision of what were to be called National Factories.[1] Under this policy, it was the Kings Norton Metal Company, a company established in 1890, that the Ministry of Munitions nominated to develop and manage the running of a new factory at Worcester, to be designated Government Cartridge Factory No.3.

The company was instructed in May 1916 to build the new factory, with the heads of agreement signed by 2 June. The site, chosen by the Kings Norton Metal Company, was in the then open countryside to the north of Worcester City and approved by the Ministry of Munitions.[2] The reasons for choosing the site were the good communications back to the parent company in Birmingham by a mainline railway which ran through the site, an adjoining canal, and the ability to tap into a nearby source of labour. In those days before motorways and bypasses, the road connections from Blackpole to Birmingham were less convenient than now, but were still reasonably direct via what later became designated as the A38 Bristol to Birmingham Trunk Road, which passed through Droitwich and Bromsgrove and on into Birmingham via the Bristol Road. Consequently, some 67½ acres of land straddling the railway line and located to the north of Worcester were compulsorily purchased under the provisions of the Defence of the Realm Act (DORA), largely (51 acres) from the trustees of the Wall family (which had been extensive landowners in Worcestershire), with some from Lord Hindlip (16½ acres). (See Fig. 2.1 for the extent and location of the site.) DORA, which had been enacted at the outset of the First World War and amended a number of times during it as the move towards total war became necessary, gave the government far-reaching powers of control over the ownership and use of land and buildings, control over the employment of people, whether in civilian life or in the armed forces, and the censorship of newspaper reporting.

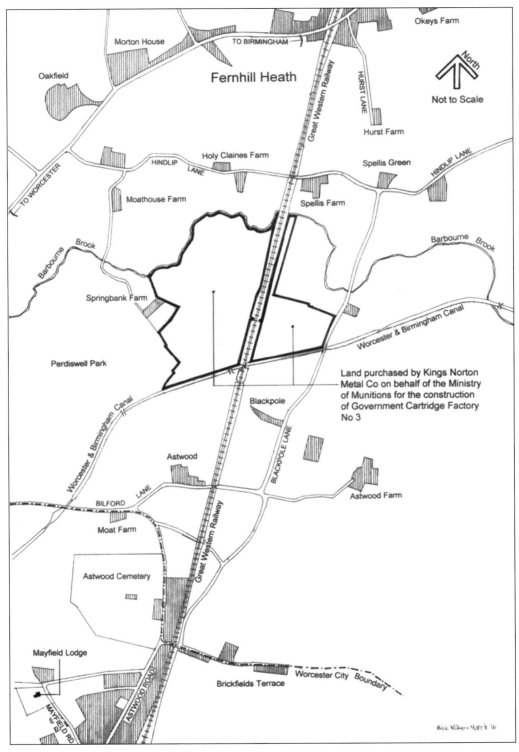

Fig. 2.1 Blackpole and environs, 1916

6

The site was purchased in August 1916 and cost £7,000 (about £500,000 in today's money). The Ministry of Munitions was to meet all the costs of the new factory, including the subsequent building, equipping and production costs, the Kings Norton Metal Company acting as its agent and being responsible for purchasing the land, designing and overseeing the construction of the buildings, and the subsequent management of production at the factory. The estimated cost of building the factory was £227,000 at 1916 prices, although this would increase until, in March 1918, the total expenditure for Blackpole had reached £289,700. Construction of the buildings and infrastructure at Blackpole was completed by February 1917 and production of small arms ammunition components began soon after. The largest building, called the bullet shop, measured 300 by almost 250 feet. Both a standard gauge railway siding from the main line into the site and a complex of light railway lines (60 centimetre or 2 foot gauge) within the site were provided to facilitate the import of raw materials, their movement around the site and the export of finished components. A canal wharf was constructed later.[3] (See Fig. 2.9 for the layout of the site.)

The development of the site at Blackpole was not without its problems, adequate water and electricity supplies being particularly difficult to provide. The site was then located in the administrative area of Droitwich Rural District, and would be so until local government boundary changes after the Second World War included Blackpole within the boundary of Worcester City. A water supply could not be provided by the Rural District Council and an approach was consequently made to Worcester City Council to provide this service. However, this was complicated by the fact that local government legislation allowed for provision of services by the City Council only within its own boundaries. This therefore required special arrangements to be made and agreement was finally made in September 1916. Arrangements to supply electricity took a little longer, but the Board of Trade authority for a supply to be made by the Shropshire, Worcestershire and Staffordshire Electric Power Company was received in January 1917, Worcester City Council laying the supply cable at a cost of £14,000. Although Droitwich Rural District Council had been party to the agreement, it was insistent that the surface of the approach road under which the pipes and cable were to be laid was made good. Clearly local government was watching potential calls on its expenditure even then! In addition to the mains water supply, Kings Norton Metal Company opened negotiations with the Worcester and Birmingham Canal Company to abstract and return water to the canal, presumably for cooling purposes in the manufacturing process, but no report of the outcome of these negotiations has been found.[4]

Press coverage of construction of the new factory was very circumspect given the provisions of DORA, but nevertheless reports of City Council meetings in local newspapers made discreet references to the new factory and the need for expenditure on services. For example, providing an adequate supply of electricity was to cost the City Council a further £12,595 for works and plant to provide the extra power, but since, by January 1917, when the matter was considered by the Council's Electricity Committee, work on the construction of the factory was well advanced, the magnanimous view of the members was that they should do something for the ultimate advantage of the city,

Blackpole No.3 Government Cartridge Factory under construction in 1916.
Top: Fig. 2.2 This appears to be of the front elevation taken from the north-east.
Note the wooden scaffold poles then in use.
Middle: Fig. 2.3 This photograph appears to be of the same elevation taken from the opposite
end and in a more advanced state of construction. Note that new bricks were delivered loosely
in 1916, and not on neat pallets as now.
Bottom: Fig. 2.4 The image immediately above appears to have been taken from the east side of
the railway embankment, looking north-eastwards at the main building.
(Courtesy of Worcestershire Archive and Archaeology Service)

quite apart from the interim value of the receipts for the electricity. It was also thought that the establishment of the factory, with anything from 1,500 to 3,000 hands, would result in excellent revenue, and could lead to the setting up of other factories in the area. The city's hydro-electric power station was then sited in the buildings – which can still be seen – adjacent to the old bridge at Powick.[5]

During the period in which the factory at Blackpole was being built, the Streets Committee of the Worcester City Council recommended that the full council should consider the effect of the new building on the locality, and the necessity of obtaining a planning scheme to ensure the proper laying out of the area. It was expected that before such a report was prepared, the factory and many workmen's dwellings would be erected. Attention was drawn to the fact that this was the first opportunity that the City Council had of presenting a town planning scheme, and that assuming that the area would at some stage become part of the city, the council should lose no chance of

Fig. 2.5 An inside view of the large building to the east of the railway, under construction in 1916. The complex roof structure of wooden lattice construction, generally known as Belfast Trusses and normally associated with the aircraft hangars of the First World War period, would provide large spans of uninterrupted space. Here the trusses are supported on a grid pattern of vertical steel joists. (Courtesy of Worcestershire Archive and Archaeology Service)

Fig. 2.6 *A view to the north, off the railway embankment, of the western half of the completed Blackpole factory. What was later to be designated Building 11, which still survives on the site, can be seen in the background, on the right, with Building 55 being the square plan, double pitched roofed building in the middle-ground. One of the propellant storage buildings, with its surrounding earth protective bund, can just be glimpsed in the background, above the nearest building. (Courtesy of Worcestershire Archive and Archaeology Service)*

Fig. 2.7 *Another view, off the railway embankment, of the west side of the completed Blackpole site, with what appears to be the butts wall of a short 25-yard shooting range on the left, presumably used for testing assembled and filled cartridges. The security fencing in the foreground is not very substantial and was perhaps only temporary, being chestnut paling surmounted by triple strands of barbed wire. There appears to be an attempt at cultivating the soil in the foreground, possibly to supply produce for the canteen.*
(Courtesy of Worcestershire Archive and Archaeology Service)

making the district as good as possible.[6] The council therefore agreed to the preparation of a town planning scheme in order to ensure the proper laying out and development of the land in the neighbourhood of the factory. The task was delegated to the City Engineer and Town Clerk working through the Plans Sub-Committee of the Streets Committee to complete a scheme. The initial task was to submit an application to the Local Government Board, which had to be convinced that there was a case for making such a scheme, a process which would involve inquiries, reports and notices, leading to a hearing of objections. The engineer submitted a plan to the sub-committee for consideration showing the area to be included within the scheme, which apparently incorporated a wide belt stretching for some distance into the county and including portions of Droitwich, Pershore and Martley Rural Districts. So began a lengthy process to produce a planning scheme.[7]

Despite the awareness of the number of jobs to be created, there is no evidence that any new housing was specifically built for the workforce during the First World War, and it is assumed that the majority of the incoming workforce was billeted in the existing housing stock. The nearby Brickfields estate, for example, was not built until the 1920s.[8]

Fig. 2.8 View southwards of the new railway siding sloping steeply down from the main Worcester to Birmingham railway line to the Blackpole factory, which at the time appears to be still under construction. The signal box, visible in the distance, was also new, and would be necessary to stop main line services when munitions trains were shunted to and from the main line. When complete the siding doubled back on itself and over the cleared land in the foreground to directly enter a yet to be constructed covered loading bay, which would adjoin the railway embankment.
(Courtesy of Worcestershire Archive and Archaeology Service)

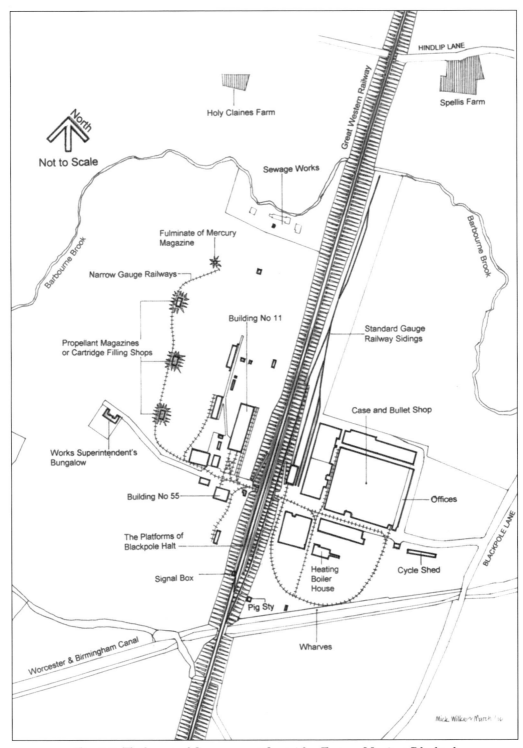

Fig. 2.9 The layout of Government Cartridge Factory No. 3 at Blackpole

Fig. 2.10 A general view of the eastern part of the completed Blackpole complex, taken from the railway bridge over the canal in June 1917, and looking to the north-east. Prominent in the picture is the chimney of the boiler house which was used to heat the factory buildings. Also apparent is a small and rudimentary wharf on the far canal side.
(Courtesy of Worcestershire Archive and Archaeology Service)

Fig. 2.11 The newly opened Blackpole factory in June 1917, with Ministry of Munitions police in the foreground. This view is of the main building looking from the main entrance to the site from Blackpole Lane, and shows the fenestration on the east face of the building, which is still much the same today.
(Courtesy of Worcestershire Archive and Archaeology Service)

Running the factory

The new national small arms ammunition factories were intended to manufacture .303 Mk VII ammunition, and the Blackpole factory started to produce this type of ammunition in February 1917. However, the Minister of Munitions was empowered to alter the type of ammunition if necessary, with the costs of changing the production machinery being charged to the ministry. Although representatives of the minister could enter the factories and make suggestions regarding the management, they were not to interfere with the control of a factory by the appointed company. Consequently, the appointed company was to hire and pay the staff engaged at the factory, including those employed in supervision and organisation. The company was also responsible for training the employees at agreed costs, these being met by the ministry. However, the raw materials used at the factory for production of ammunition were to be purchased directly from, or through, the ministry.

The initial production rate for cartridges at Blackpole was set at 500,000 rounds per week to begin with, rising to 6,000,000 per week as soon as possible. The standard

Fig. 2.12 The cartridge case shop in June 1917. Cartridge cases required a number of punch operations to form the complex shape in brass, and the heavy flywheels, seen here, were necessary to maintain the momentum of the presses during these operations. Driven by speeding overhead belts and pulleys, health and safety considerations were clearly not of great concern in those days, in what seems to have been an extremely dangerous work environment.
(Courtesy of Worcestershire Archive and Archaeology Service)

Fig. 2.13 *It is unclear what process is going on in this picture, but the part formed cartridge cases in the trays in the foreground suggests that the large drums might be used for annealing the metal in the cases before the punching process is continued.*
(Courtesy of Worcestershire Archive and Archaeology Service)

Fig. 2.14 *Another view of the crowded bullet case shop with the complex cats cradle effect of the multiple drive belts for the machinery.*
(Courtesy of Worcestershire Archive and Archaeology Service)

price for the production of cartridges was set at 120 shillings per 1,000 cartridges delivered, while the management fee for the factory was set at 2 shillings 6 pence per 1,000 accepted cartridges, although a bonus could be paid for economical working.

While the new National Factories were still under construction, the Russian government requested that the Ministry of Munitions provide 7.62mm calibre ammunition for use in their standard service rifle, the Moisin Nagant, and consequently two of the Government Cartridge Factories (those run by the Birmingham Metal and Munitions Company and the Woolwich Arsenal) were converted to produce the Russian ammunition. By the end of the year, it was decided by the ministry to increase the amount of ammunition supplied to the Russians and that the Kings Norton Company would be required to change the tooling to produce 7.62mm cartridges at Blackpole.

In January 1917, and before production had started at Blackpole, it was further decided by the ministry to halve the production rates originally planned at all the cartridge factories; consequently Blackpole was to reduce production to 3 million cartridges per week. As a result of this change of policy, all the cartridge factories were to reduce their hours of working to a day shift only, instead of both day and night shift

Fig. 2.15 A view of the tool room at Blackpole where women under the supervision of skilled engineers are using lathes to create the tools necessary for punching the cartridges and bullets to shape. The lathe in the foreground appears to have one such tool still in the chuck.
(Courtesy of Worcestershire Archive and Archaeology Service)

working. This completely changed the conditions under which the managing firms were to produce ammunition and changes to the original agreements were requested from the ministry, not least because the profits the managing companies had expected to make were considerably reduced and considered to be 'a most inadequate return for the labour and services involved'. Kings Norton Metal Company consequently proposed a revised price of 144 shillings per 1,000 cartridges, and a management fee of 3 shillings 6 pence per 1,000 cartridges in light of the difference in profitability. It was further proposed that the economy bonus should be increased. The negotiations on the changes to the agreements proved to be long and complicated and it was not until September 1918 that settlements were finally made. Although starting production later than other cartridge factories, the output from the Blackpole factory reached the planned production by October 1917 of 3,000,000 cartridges per week with no rejections by the Inspection Department. This performance was apparently largely due to the energy and resource of the manager, Jack Hewson Needham.

Fig. 2.16 Clearly identified as the bullet shop from the storage barrels in the foreground, this image portrays very well the crowded working conditions of the women workers in this part of the factory. The noise generated by the many presses can only be imagined. There are several points to note: the coils of shiny metal in the foreground which is probably the cupro-nickel alloy used to form the bullet casings; the small number of supervisory, and probably skilled, experienced, men in the background; again the multiplicity of belts and pulleys driving the presses, where a moment's inattention could have resulted in a nasty accident.
(Courtesy of Worcestershire Archive and Archaeology Service)

.303 Mk VII ammunition

The first .303 cartridges were manufactured in 1889 for the new Lee-Metford magazine-fed service rifle which was replacing the single shot Martini-Henry rifles of Zulu War fame. The new cartridges incorporated a round-nosed, cupro-nickel jacketed, lead-filled projectile or bullet, with a rimmed brass cartridge case. The propellant for this Mark I version of the .303 round was black powder, but this was quickly replaced by cordite to achieve a smokeless discharge on firing. Subsequently nitro-cellulose was also used as the propellant. Each change in the .303 cartridge and bullet form or propellant was given a new mark number, the Mark VII round with a pointed bullet being introduced in 1910. (Fig. 2.18 illustrates the form and components of a Mk VII .303 cartridge.) This version of the .303 ammunition remained in use, with various adaptations, by the British armed services until replaced by the NATO standard calibre ammunition of 7.62mm in the 1970s. The identification markings, or head stamps, of the Mk VII .303 calibre cartridge produced during both world wars at Blackpole are BE or B and E with the War Department broad arrow between, or F3 denoting Cartridge Factory No.3. Other markings can include Z for nitro-cellulose filling or T for tracer.[11]

First World War Russian 7.92mm calibre · Mark VII .303 inch calibre

Second World War Mark VII .303 inch calibre · 9mm calibre

Fig. 2.17 Types of cartridges produced at Blackpole in two world wars. (Photo courtesy of Malcolm Atkin)

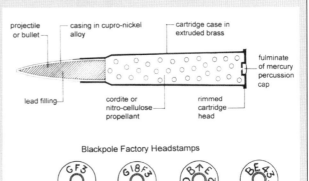

Fig. 2.18 The components of the Mk VII .303 cartridge and the Blackpole factory headstamps

The Blackpole factory was able to produce complete cartridges, which included filling with the propellant (explosive). The buildings that were used for the filling process have not been definitively identified, but three small buildings on the west side of the site (see Figs. 2.6 and 2.9) are indicated with a protective earth bund around them, which suggests that this is where the process took place. That the construction of bungalows in that vicinity by the Cadbury Company in the 1920s (see below) prevented the use of the Blackpole site for filling cartridges in the Second World War lends support to this contention.

While the factory at Blackpole was busily producing 7.62mm ammunition for the Russians, a Bolshevik inspired revolution was taking place in their country. The Tsar had abdicated in March 1917, with the country subsequently becoming a republic, and while the provisional government had wanted to continue the war against Germany, the Bolsheviks did not. After seizing power in November 1917, the Bolsheviks negotiated the end of hostilities, culminating in the signing of an armistice with Germany in December 1917. The end of the war between Russia and Germany was ratified in the Brest-Litovsk Treaty of 3 March 1918.

Given the circumstances in Russia, the Minister of Munitions reduced the required output of 7.62mm cartridges and on 7 December 1917, the Blackpole factory ceased production of this calibre ammunition.[9] Just a week later the Blackpole factory had started manufacturing .303 inch Mk VII cartridges (see the graph in Fig. 2.19). Besides the calibre of bullet changing, the cartridge for 7.62 calibre ammunition is both shorter and fatter than that of .303 (see Fig. 4), so the changes to the tooling involved in the manufacture of the two calibres and the required checking gauges, must have been substantial. Nevertheless, the factory achieved the target production by the end of the month of 3,000,000 rounds per week of .303 calibre ammunition. This rate of production was raised in February 1918 to 4,000,000 cartridges a week and, by increasing the working hours to maximum capacity by both day and night working, sacrificing the Easter and Whitsun holidays and relaxation of weekend working, to a weekly output of 9,000,000 cartridges by the end of July. By 24 August 1918, the total output of .303 calibre cartridges delivered from Blackpole was 192,418,550.

The high level of output from the Blackpole factory was recorded as being due to its excellent management throughout its history, careful organisation by the authorities, and good cooperation by its employees. The bullets turned out were also considered to be some of the best in the trade.[10]

After the Armistice on 11 November 1918, three months' notice was given by the ministry to the cartridge factories to cease production and instructions issued that no more virgin copper, spelter or nickel should be used. Consequently production tailed off in the following months, but continued in much reduced quantities beyond the government's deadline, with the Blackpole factory only being reported as closed on 5 September 1919, with Mr Needham and other staff being transferred back to the parent company in Kings Norton.

The workforce

It was intended that the new cartridge factories should be models of what could be achieved by using the smallest possible quantity of trained labour and making maximum use of women's labour. Of all the new Ministry of Munitions factories, the process of dilution of labour (see below) was carried out to its fullest extent at Blackpole, which, by May 1917 had only 4% of skilled men employed throughout the works, with 82% of the workforce being women and boys. The remainder of the workforce was provided by unskilled men. By October 1918, of the 3,235 employees, 2,462 were women.[12]

It was claimed that the efficient use of semi-skilled and unskilled labour at Blackpole and elsewhere in Ministry of Munitions factories, was achieved by a combination of scientific design of factory layout and improved management of the workforce. Whereas before the war a skilled worker would, for example, have carried out a number of machining tasks and assembly of a component, under the dilution scheme the process was broken down into a number of straightforward single tasks, each to be carried out by individually unskilled men or women, with accuracy of the work being quickly and easily checked by the use of gauges. The final assembly would then be carried out by the limited numbers of skilled workers. The improved working conditions introduced by the government included the provision of factory canteens, rest rooms, wash rooms and medical facilities.[13]

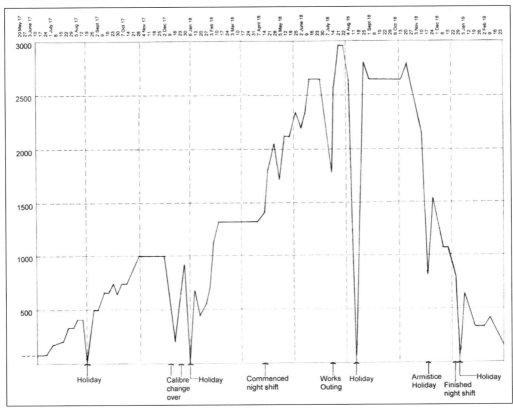

Fig. 2.19 Graph showing the employment figures for the Blackpole factory with some key events noted

Responsibility for recruiting the staff for the new factory was that of the Kings Norton Metal Company, and the minutes of the board indicate that appointment of the senior managers began in late 1916, the managing director, later superintendent, Jack Needham, and an unnamed accountant being listed on 1 December. It is likely that other managers were transferred from the parent factory in Birmingham.

The women employed in munitions work were trained in 70 centres in Britain, seven of the centres being instructional factories owned by the Ministry of Munitions which overall could accommodate 800 women at any one time. The courses lasted for six weeks.[14] It has not been possible to determine whether the Blackpole factory was one of instructional factories, but it seems likely that it was.

Although at this time there was no formal conscription procedure for bringing women workers into industry, a registration scheme was introduced in 1915 for women prepared to do such work and so release men for the armed services. The scheme proved to be ineffectual, most of the volunteering women being employed in office jobs. This changed in 1916 when conscription of men into the armed forces was introduced, and when women were more readily placed by the employment exchanges in industrial work. Many of the women recruited for the Blackpole factory were not local and a committee was established to compile lists of suitable accommodation. This system was superseded with the passing of the Billeting Act in May 1917, and a Billeting Board was established that August. The board worked in liaison with local authorities and could requisition suitable buildings to provide hostels.

Advertisements had appeared in local papers since at least January 1917 urgently seeking accommodation for war workers, aimed at householders in Worcester, Malvern, Evesham, Pershore and the surrounding area. It was said that the accommodation was required for 'thousands of workers', many of whom were said to be coming from 'good homes', and in a few weeks would be 'flocking into the locality from all parts of the country'. The advertisements appealed to all those who could possibly offer any accommodation, 'even if only for one person'. Those responding to the appeal were asked to set out concisely the number of persons they could accommodate, the price they would charge for sleeping accommodation with breakfast and supper, and whether the accommodation was to be offered to men or women.[15]

With accommodation scattered over a wide area, a significant number of the workforce came by train to the factory and in December 1917 approval was given for the construction of a halt specifically for the use of the munitions workers. This was built in early 1918 on the top of the railway embankment where it passes through the Blackpole factory site. The work was carried out by men from the factory, the halt being provided with two platforms, both 600 feet long by 12 feet wide, connected by a concrete roadway which went under a bridge in the embankment. Tragedy struck during the construction work when on Friday 22 February 1918, William Atwell, aged 26, a bricklayer from near Bristol, fell from scaffolding where he was working on constructing the platforms onto the concrete roadway. He was treated in the First Aid Room at the factory by Dr Pollard, before being taken to the Worcester Royal Infirmary in Castle Street, where he died as a result of a fractured skull. Thomas Keenlyside of the GWR Engineering Department, who was in charge of the work, said at the inquest that they were removing

Fig. 2.20 The bridge still exists under the main railway line embankment at the Blackpole site, through which the light railway used to connect the two halves of the site, and scene of the tragic accident in 1918 referred to in the text. The concrete sleepers to the right of the bridge are also remnants of the light railway, reused here to form a retaining wall for part of the embankment. Gone are the platforms above the embankment that used to form the Blackpole Halt and the standard gauge siding which sloped down this side of the embankment.
(Photo by Mick Wilks, August 2015)

staging when Atwell had slipped and fallen. A verdict of accidental death was brought by the inquest jury.[16]

Nevertheless the work was completed by May 1918. Inclined pathways led to the platforms at which trains called at eight hour intervals to coincide with staff shift changes.[17] The halt remained in being until it was demolished after the Second World War and there is now no sign of it ever having existed.

Also in 1918, piling was installed for a wharf alongside the canal. Some of those working at the factory used the canal towpath to reach the site, which resulted in complaints by the canal company over the use of what was, in effect, private property.[18]

Unfortunately, and despite extensive searches of archives, it has not been possible to find any personal memories of working at the Blackpole factory and there are no longer any living witnesses to that time.

Wages and the cost of living
Over the period of the war, food prices as well as wages more than doubled. The weekly wage rates for the munitions factories were set by the Ministry of Munitions and at the end of 1917 these stood at 24 shillings (£1.20) plus 2 shillings and 6 pence (12.5 pence) for women doing men's work, and 22 shillings (£1.10) plus a bonus for women doing what was deemed women's work if it amounted to a 48 hour week. Average earnings, however, were above these figures due to overtime and piecework. Given the

> **Easing the workload**
>
> Standing at a machine for the length of an 8 or 12 hour shift could be hard on the operator's feet and the local newspapers carried advertisements extolling the virtues of their treatment for tired and aching feet. Notable were the advertisements claiming 'how glorious, how grand TIZ makes tired, swollen, sore, perspiring feet feel', and suggesting that the tired worker, when they arrived home from work, should take off their shoes and put their 'weary, aching, burning feet in a TIZ bath'. Some of the advertisements included a sketch of a munitionette in her long smock and wearing the snood headgear, making it very clear at whom the promotion was aimed. TIZ also made similar claims for the tired soldier at the front![19]
>
> Another claim was that PEPS would stop the autumn cough getting down into the lungs, especially for munitions workers, for whom the tablet would be a defence against the damp, early morning air, on the way to or from work. It was said to be comforting, healing, and germ destroying.[20]

standardisation of wages across all the Ministry of Munitions factories, it was possible to compare production costs, which shows that the Blackpole factory had the lowest costs. This may have influenced the immediate, but short-lived, post-war government policy towards the factory.[21]

In January 1917, the *Worcester Daily Times* drew attention to the fact that the higher wages now being earned by women war workers had resulted in them being accused of extravagance, and that they were buying fur coats and having boxes of chocolates by their lathe, while those working elsewhere were underpaid and earning just 3 pence an hour or less. Both extremes, the newspaper explained, were apparently exceptions, and went on to write that the Minister of Munitions had in fact done more for women workers in 15 months than any other authority had done in 15 years. As early as October 1915 he had published a circular with the keynote phrase, 'equal pay for equal work'. By this order, women were to be paid the same piece rates as men. These terms were applied at once in the National Factories, but were only recommendations for private establishments. A special arbitration panel had also been established by the minister to deal exclusively with women's wages. The newspaper pointed out that the effect of these arrangements was to secure for the majority of women and girls engaged on munitions work a decent living wage, and when on piecework, earnings undreamt of by the average women worker in pre-war times.[22]

War workers badges
The Order of the White Feather was a group of women who presented men not in the uniform of the fighting services with a white feather as a symbol of their cowardice. With the white feather campaign becoming a serious nuisance, the government proposed the issue of War Workers lapel badges to be worn by male munitions workers to indicate that they were doing their bit towards the war effort. Badges were initially issued by the Admiralty and the War Office, but the Munitions Act included a section authorising the Ministry of Munitions to issue such badges to its own workforce. Separate badges were

Fig. 2.21 War workers badges of two world wars.
Top left: First 'official' badge issued in 1915
with blue and white enamel finish.
Top middle: The all brass 'economy' badge of later in 1915.
Top right: The women's triangular all brass badge
issued in 1916.
Left: Second World War bronze war worker's badge issued
specifically for what was then Royal Ordnance Factory
No. 20 at Blackpole.
(Images courtesy of Malcolm Atkin)

issued to volunteer male war workers, these being skilled workers from other industries who had volunteered to work in a munitions factory. If such a man was posted away from his home locality, he would receive a subsistence allowance in addition to his former level of pay. Figure 2.21 illustrates the various badges issued to war workers. The official badges issued in 1915 were colourfully enamelled, but these were soon replaced by a plain brass badge when the sheer scale of supplying the badges became apparent. (A badge specific to Blackpole ROF No. 20 issued in the Second World War is also illustrated.)

Many companies issued their own design of workers badge during the First World War, but these were declared to be illegal in the summer of 1915 and consequently were of little value when men were being called up for service in the armed forces after compulsory service was introduced in 1916. By that time, official badges had already been described in a War Office circular intended specifically to help recruiting officers recognise the correct badges. It also became necessary to ensure that a badge was not being worn by someone not entitled to it so as to avoid military service and relevant rules were issued under the provisions of the Munitions of War Act. As a result a wearer had to be in a certified occupation, which was defined as employed in the production of any commodity directly required for the fulfilment of any contract with the Ministry of Munitions, War Office or Admiralty, and the transfer of badges from one person to another became illegal. In addition, anyone leaving certified employment could not retain his badge. To do so would be a criminal offence and penalties for breaking the rules could be up to six months in gaol, with or without hard labour, or a £100 fine. If the offence could be proved to be assisting the enemy, the death penalty could be imposed.

Some of the women munitions workers considered that they too should have a badge, but initially this was seen as unnecessary and too costly. When Lloyd George gave his support to the scheme in 1916, however, a simple triangular badge was introduced.

Concern for the welfare of munitions workers

Mr and Mrs Arthur Carlton, the then Mayor and Mayoress of Worcester City, made available their former residence of Mayfield Lodge, also apparently called Ravenscroft, as a club for girl workers at Blackpole. This large house used to stand on the corner of Mayfield Road and Green Lane, in the Rainbow Hill area of Worcester, a mile or so from the factory (see the bottom left corner of Figure 2.1 for the location). The cost of adapting half the house to its new use was met partly by donations, and partly by funds from the Church Extension Fund. Recreation rooms were created on the ground floor with a 'rest room' upstairs furnished with settees, armchairs, writing tables and materials, as well as the nucleus of a library, with papers, periodicals and magazines. Also upstairs was an oratory with an altar, prayer desk and hassocks, together with a committee room where meetings could be held. The club was formally opened on Saturday 3 June 1917 by the mayoress, in readiness for the girls who were expected to arrive shortly from 'far and wide', although their number was uncertain.[23] Clearly, the mayor, mayoress and the local church authorities expected the girls to lead a well ordered life! Sadly, not all the girls were paragons of virtue and the Baptist Women's League had already become concerned about swearing by munitions girls.[24] Perhaps it was this concern for the girls' morals that inspired the mayor and mayoress to make their offer in the first place. Mayfield Lodge has now gone, the site having been recently redeveloped with several residential apartment blocks.

Fig. 2.22 A very serious group of 'munitionettes' at Blackpole during the First World War. Only one of the women has been identified and this is Cecily Ida Probert in the centre of the second row wearing the lighter smock with the dark armbands, which probably denote some supervisory status. (Courtesy of Mr Greenow of Worcester)

The welfare of both men and women munitions workers also exercised the mind of the bishop of Worcester, who called a special meeting of the Diocesan Finance Board which unanimously agreed that a welfare fund of £10,000 should be collected in the light of the 'invasion' of the diocese by an army of men and women working at the munitions factories. He was in no doubt that 'anyone well acquainted with the munitions workers would support the need for Christian patriots to be up and doing on behalf of the happiness, spiritual and temporal of these people, who were giving themselves to national defence'. He believed that supporting such work was as paramount as subscribing to any of the soldiers' comforts, and that the munitions workers should not be degraded in body or soul. Quite how the Diocesan Board was going to utilise the money is not explained or, later, how his campaign fared![25]

'Combing out' men for the Army and Navy
1917 saw the War Office making further demands for men for the Army and Navy, and the Ministry of Munitions undertook to provide a 'considerable number' of the 500,000 men required. Consequently the possession of a badge and certificate issued previously could no longer guarantee that a worker would avoid military service as a 'combing out' process began. Henceforth, protection certificates would only be issued to men who were engaged in the construction of ships and munitions in occupations scheduled as being essential. By this process the government hoped to achieve full and economic use of the manpower available while, at the same time, maintaining the Army in the field and dealing with the U-boat menace. Protection certificates were now to be issued by Munitions Area Recruiting Offices to all munitions workers entitled to them under the relevant schedule. This new procedure was not intended to supersede exceptions to military service given by Military Tribunals.[26] How this combing out process affected the workforce at Blackpole is not recorded.

Resolution of disputes
Any disputes between those employed and the employers were dealt with by the Worcester Munitions Court which had been specifically established to resolve employment issues. A sign of relative unanimity at the Blackpole Factory is the few times that staff from the factory appeared before the court. One such occasion, however, occurred on Friday 21 December 1918, after the Armistice, when William Inett of Worcester claimed wages in lieu of a week's notice from the Kings Norton Metal Company. Apparently on 9 September he had informed Mr H.G. Hills, the inspector of the loading department, where he was working, that he was ill with chronic rheumatism and was not fit to work. He saw the works doctor the day after and obtained a certificate, but did not produce it until two days afterwards. Inett alleged that the firm had dismissed him without notice, which the firm denied, saying that he left of his own accord. The firm also complained that the claim had not been made in a reasonable time. Judgement was given by the Munitions Court for the complainant for the full amount that he was able to claim: £3 2 shillings. The labour superintendent to the company said that he would appeal against it, but it is not known if he did. The court comprised of Mr E.G.M. Carmichael

(Chairman), Mr J.A. Woolley (Masters' Assessor) and Mr T. Grimmer (Workmen's Assessor).[27]

Further evidence of the unanimity at Blackpole had come earlier when a strike in July 1918 by munitions workers in the Midlands did not spread to the Blackpole factory. The dispute stemmed from an embargo being put on certain firms restricting the employment of skilled workers in engineering, and extending the use of semi-skilled and unskilled workmen. The numbers of skilled men striking, or threatening to strike, were significant, with 18,000 men in Coventry ceasing work and with men in Birmingham, Manchester and Lincoln threatening to unless the embargo was lifted. Subsequently, some 120,000 men and women in Birmingham and district, roughly 80% of munitions workers, went on strike. The Secretary of the Joint Committee of the Engineering Trades Unions made it clear in a statement that the strikers in the Birmingham and Coventry areas had not listened to their leaders, and consequently strike pay would not be distributed. The dispute was settled by the government in a novel but ruthless way. The Prime Minister considered that the men had ceased work, not in pursuance of a trade dispute, but in an endeavour to force the government to change the national policy essential to the prosecution of the war. He made it clear that, whilst millions of their fellow countrymen were hourly facing danger and death for their country, the men then on strike had been granted exemption from these perils only because their services were considered of more value to the state in the workshop than in the Army. The government consequently declared that all men wilfully absent from their work on or after Monday 29 July, would be deemed to have voluntarily placed themselves outside the area of the munitions industries. Their protection certificates would cease to have effect from that day and they would become liable to the provisions of the Military Service Acts. Apparently National Service officials were busy preparing forms for issue on the Monday calling upon strikers to present themselves for examination immediately, should they decide not to return to work!

A resolution by the Worcester Branch of the Comrades of the Great War took a similar approach to the government, declaring that the engineers then on strike should be sent to France forthwith and skilled men in the trenches released to take their place. Further, the branch pledged themselves to support the government in any action it might take in compelling these favoured few to do their duty to their country. They suggested that discharged men of Worcester and the county were prepared to undertake any work which was hitherto performed by 'these slackers'![28]

Air raids in the Midlands and air raid precautions
Air raids by German aircraft on Britain began in December 1914, with an attack on Dover by relatively small aircraft carrying only a small bombload. More serious raids began when Zeppelin airships capable of carrying greater bombloads over longer distances were used. The first Zeppelin raid on the West Midlands came one night at the end of January 1916. Responsibility for air raid precautions had been given to local councils and the policy, which, when a warning of an imminent raid was received, was to impose lighting restrictions on a potential target area and by means of bells and horns

encourage the local population to seek shelter in cellars or under railway arches or to disperse out into the countryside. There were no shelters provided at this time of the type introduced during the Second World War and it is assumed that the workforce at Blackpole, on receiving such a warning, would leave the factory and seek shelter in the best way available to them. In fact the factory was not attacked during the Great War, the nearest bomb to the site being one thought to have been dropped from a Zeppelin at Kidderminster on 31 January 1916. The bomb did not explode and was found in 1939, in the Worcester Road area of the town.[29]

The effect of the Armistice

Most of the works in Worcester gave their workforce the day off on Tuesday 12 November 1918 to allow a celebration of the signing of the Armistice which had occurred the day before. The Blackpole factory was no exception. Although some men turned up for work in the morning, many gave up after an hour and joined the celebrations. Work was to be resumed on the following day.

The Armistice brought a number of immediate benefits to the local population which were announced by the Chief Constable in response to a Home Office instruction. The masking of public lights was ended, as was the shading of home and shop lights, whilst fireworks and bonfires would be permitted again, all of these restrictions having been introduced as a means of thwarting the Zeppelin raiders. Public clocks were allowed to strike and bells to be rung at night again, since the threat of an enemy invasion had now passed. In addition, regulations requiring the closing of restaurants at 9.30pm, and theatres at 10.30pm were suspended.[30]

The Ministry of Munitions reacted with commendable speed to the Armistice by giving official notice to contractors, sub-contractors and workers on 13 November that the task was now to transform industry from war to peace. It was seen to be inevitable that there would be disturbance and dislocation to both the industries and workshops, and that large numbers of people would have to change employment and in many cases, where they lived. To recognise the good work that had been done to bring the war to a victorious conclusion, the government intended to limit hardship and waste and issued the following instructions to all firms engaged on work for the Ministry of Munitions:

> There should be no immediate general discharge of munitions workers.
> All workers who desired to withdraw from the industry or leave for any reason or who could be absorbed elsewhere should be released at once.
> Production on munitions contracts should be reduced by stopping all overtime, temporarily suspending systems of payment by results, and reducing hours to not less than half the previous hours in a normal working week. In any case the weekly earnings of anyone should not fall below the following amounts:
>> men of 18 and over - 30 shillings,
>> boys under 18 - 15 shillings,
>> women of 18 and over - 25 shillings,
>> girls under 18 - 12 shillings and 6 pence.

These earnings were to be made up by the employer who would be reimbursed by the state. Every effort was to be made to avoid unemployment.

Free rail warrants were to be issued through the employment exchanges for those wishing to travel to their homes or places of new employment.

Where discharges of munitions workers was being contemplated, the management of firms was encouraged to work in close cooperation with employment exchanges in order to facilitate return to their homes and re-absorption into industry.[31]

Lloyd George followed these instructions with an announcement to a conference of employers and workers' associations that during this transition period and with the high cost of living, the present level of wages should be maintained for six months. To facilitate the transfer of workers, employment exchanges were to be given 14 days' notice of the number of workers to be dispensed with, together with their names and addresses and previous occupation. The order of discharge was to be:

those who were not industrial workers before and willing to go,
those who could go to their previous occupations or to vacancies,
the bad timekeepers,
workers who had not served a given amount of time, were brought in from other districts and were making a heavy demand on transport services.[32]

The performance of women workers

At the end of the war, the National Employers Federation assessed and reported on the performance of women in the engineering and metal industries and drew comparisons with the performance of men. It makes interesting reading. In connection with cartridge production, it was found that women not only produced a quality which was the equal of men, but that in terms of output they could equal that of men, and in some cases produced 20% more. For labouring tasks, although the Employers Federation considered that three women were the equivalent of two men, it was found that for light repetitive work women were both more efficient and more productive. Unfortunately post-war Britain did not provide the future that women workers may have expected and in the first two weeks after the Armistice, some 113,000 women were discharged. Too little thought had been given to what might have been done to adapt work for them or to the provision of training to avoid unemployment.[33]

The departure of Jack Hewson Needham

As has been mentioned above, Jack Needham was clearly a good manager of the Blackpole factory and this was reflected when, in December 1918, the remaining workforce (many had already left the factory) decided to show their appreciation before there was a general dispersal of the staff. A concert and dance was held in the large canteen at the works, together with refreshments provided by the Canteen Manager, Mr Askew. Employees from all departments were present and, during an interval in the concert, a number of gifts were presented to Jack Needham by Lewis Godfrey of the Order

Department. He praised the superintendent's energy, hard work and perseverance in the face of many difficulties which, with the cooperation of all departments, had achieved greater results than had been anticipated. Although the policy was to achieve maximum output from the factory, Needham was said to have also believed in the workers' comfort, which was reflected in the parting gifts. These were an illuminated address, a silver salver and a gold cigarette case, both of the latter suitably engraved. The illuminated address was a colourful work of art of floral design and incorporating the names of various colonies, interwoven with a belt of machine gun cartridges and a picture of a girl working one of the machines. In the address on it, reference was made to Jack Needham having returned from Chile to England in response to the national call for service and having thrown his energy into the production of small arms ammunition. The address also included a revealing list of the departmental managers and their signatures. These were: J. Aldridge (Tool Shop), C. Bovis (Carpenters' Shop), H.E. Clive (Case Shop), J.W. Devon (Electrician), F. Finan (Drawing Office), Lewis H. Godfrey (Order Department), William Green Hough (Bullet Shop), J.B. Gurney (Police), William Hewitt (Labour), J. Herbert Hicklin (Laboratory), W.H. Higginbottom (Accountant), W.D. Hills (Inspection and Loading), J.E. Hornblower (Machine Shop), H. Jones (Offices), A.W. Linegar (Stores), Robert M. Moody (Wages), W. Pretty (Plant), T. Edgar Smith (Costs), H.M.S. Sutor (Welfare), H. Bernard Wellbank (Cashier) and William A. Wigley Smith (also Offices). The address, dated 6 December 1918, was framed with oak taken from an old shaking barrel from the Annealing Shop, where it had been in use in filling cartridges. The frame had been made in the Carpenters' Shop.

Jack Needham was apparently touched by the presentation and in his response said that he had been out of the country for 20 years before his return. He praised the workforce for their loyal cooperation in making the factory so successful, and confirmed that his appeals for extra effort had been met with a magnificent response. Consequently, he thought that workers were entitled to share in the expression of satisfaction of the Ministry of Munitions in the way that the factory had been conducted. He finished by thanking the workers for their cooperation in maintaining law and order, and reflected on the fact that he was struggling with the 'reconstruction' (by which he presumably meant the reuse of the site and buildings), and hoped to make an announcement about the factory before long.[34]

3 BLACKPOLE BETWEEN THE WARS

With the signing of the Armistice on 11 November 1918, the demand for small arms ammunition reduced considerably and the British government turned its thoughts to the peacetime requirements for ammunition production. The future of the Blackpole factory then became the subject of much muddled thinking by the Ministry of Munitions. Its record of quality and rate of production marked out the factory for continued production of small arms ammunition, should production at Woolwich be discontinued. Consequently, the factory was one of four of the government's National Factories shortlisted by the ministry for further use. Later, an alternative use for Blackpole as a government factory for the production of electrical and brass fittings, including press work of radiator tubes for use in aircraft, was considered. This was then discounted because it was thought that the factory would be competing with private industry, but it was decided that for the first year after the Armistice Blackpole should continue in small arms ammunition.[1]

Despite this decision, it became clear that the factory was being rundown by the government before the year was finished, and this was reflected in the social function described at the end of the last chapter. In July 1919, concern for the workforce was expressed in Parliament by the Right Honourable J. Davidson, who asked the Parliamentary Secretary of the Ministry of Munitions whether he was aware of the numerous discharges taking place at Government Cartridge Factory No.3, Blackpole; that many of the men employed at the factory had come from other districts and had settled in Worcester with their families; that the lack of information as to the future of the factory and possibility of re-employment was causing inconvenience; and whether it was the intention to close the factory down entirely, or whether there was the prospect of re-engaging the discharged men on other work.

The Parliamentary Secretary, Mr James Hope, said that it was proposed that the factory should be retained for the present under government control but, in view of the large stocks of small arms ammunition held by the military, he was afraid that there was no likelihood that manufacturing would be resumed in the near future. It was probable that the factory would be needed for storage, in which case he feared the number of employees would not be large.[2]

Closure of the factory came on 5 September 1919, with the transfer of Mr Needham and several staff back to the Kings Norton parent factory.[3] For his contribution to the success of the Blackpole factory, Jack Needham had been awarded the OBE, gazetted on 30 March 1920.[4]

The workforce were, however, not to receive such recognition for their efforts, the Ministry of Munitions deciding that they would receive no medal, despite a promise from Lord Kitchener in 1915 that they would. The reason given was that since Lord Kitchener's announcement, the resources of the whole country had been devoted to war work and it had been found difficult to differentiate between the various classes of war workers at home.[5]

By November 1919 the Minister of War considered that the factory should be put on the market for disposal, either by sale or lease, at the same time as providing for the storage of munitions machinery on part of the site and for the speedy reconversion of the site and buildings to munitions production should a national emergency again arise. Under the terms of their original contract with the Ministry of Munitions, the Kings Norton Metal Company could purchase the factory at a 5% discount if the government decided to dispose of it. There is no record of the company considering this option.

Advertisements for the sale of the factory appeared in local newspapers on 20 December 1919, noting that the site was to be sold by tender in one lot and subject to unspecified conditions. The advertisements described a site of about 69 acres divided into two by the Great Western Railway (Oxford and Worcester Line), with the main buildings constructed of brick with ruberoid or asbestos slate roofs. The buildings comprised a case and bullet shop, with offices and small buildings adjoining of 86,332 square feet super (i.e. as measured from the outside of the building); an annealing shop with additions of 19,273 sq ft; carpenters' shop with power and tractor house of 11,391 sq ft; boiler house of 4,428 sq ft; canteen of 16,226 sq ft; inspection and general store, loading dock and small additions of 42,411 sq ft; and a main shop of 8,060 sq ft. The remainder of the buildings included a manager's bungalow, cycle shed, laundry, stores, female dressing rooms, cap factory, and magazine. The total floor area of the buildings was said to be 230,000 sq ft super. Low pressure steam heating was provided in the shops, with electric heating in the offices. A public supply of gas and electricity was available, and water from a corporation main. Private railway sidings connected to the main line were listed, but there is no mention of the narrow gauge track within the site. The Worcester and Birmingham Canal with a loading wharf is described as affording good facilities for water-borne traffic. Forms of tender, conditions of sale and a plan were to be obtained from the Controller, Land and Factories Section of the Disposal Board, at Charing Cross Buildings, Embankment, London.[6]

After its closure, it was recorded that in May 1920 there were still 25 staff at the factory, presumably to provide some security and to work on care and maintenance of the buildings.[7]

Post-war industrial unrest and its effect on Blackpole factory
The Trade Union movement had grown in both size and efficiency during the First World War. Membership had doubled to over 8 million by 1919, and a Triple Alliance of the three main unions – engineering, transport and coal mining – had been formed in 1916. Disillusionment with the post-war world, which had not lived up to the promise of creating a land fit for heroes, led to increased militancy by the working classes and a mood for strike action. Transport workers were the first to come out, but threats by the

Triple Alliance to foment a more general strike gave the impression that Britain was on the edge of a social revolution. In the summer of 1920 the coal miners asked for support from the other members of the Alliance in their desire to strike for better wages and a reduction in the price of coal. A miners' strike was called in April 1921, resulting in the government declaring a state of emergency.

As part of its response the government raised a special volunteer defence force for a service period of up to 90 days. The purpose of the force was to maintain law and order, and assist in protecting those who were employed on essential services without which it was predicted that people would starve. The force could be required to serve in England, Scotland or Wales, but not in Northern Ireland or overseas. The rates of pay were to be the then current Army rates of 2 shillings and 9 pence a day for a private, with rations and accommodation provided. Married men would receive married men's allowance. Men in receipt of a disability pension could join if the medical officer passed them and would continue to receive their pension in addition to pay. Old ex-servicemen, except those in the Territorial Force, would receive an allowance of £5 on completion of their service. Every man would enlist as a private, but promotion to acting rank would be made according to requirements. Service in the ranks was limited to men between 18 and 40 years of age, but men of up to 45 could be accepted for appointment as a sergeant or warrant officer. Recruits were invited to enlist at any drill hall. If the militaristic tone of the response seems excessive, it must be remembered that there recently had been an armed rising in Ireland and a Bolshevik Revolution in Russia; the government feared something similar on the UK mainland.

Lord Coventry made an appeal on 10 April, inviting all loyal citizens of the county to enrol in the special defence force, Worcestershire being asked to raise two battalions of infantry and one battery of field artillery. Meanwhile the Mayor of Worcester, Charles Edwards, specifically asked for men from Worcester to join a battery of Field

Fig. 3.1 A parade outside the Blackpole factory of the special 90-day volunteer defence force recruited in 1921 to deal with potential public order problems by striking miners. Some men have uniforms and are probably serving territorial soldiers, while the majority are still wearing their civilian clothing. The front rank appear to have just been given the order to fix bayonets and are reaching to their left side. (Courtesy of the Cadbury Archive, Mondelez International)

Artillery based on the Drill Hall at No.24 Southfield Street, and to form two companies of infantry based on the Territorial force's Drill Hall at No.16 Silver Street. He also appealed to those citizens who were employers, to release men to serve and to keep their places open until they returned. By mid-April apparently 50% of the required men had been enrolled.

There had been a ready response from ex-officers, with Colonel P.M. Tomkinson appointed to command the 7th Battalion, Colonel W.R. Chichester to command the 8th Battalion, and Colonel A.T. Anderson CMG to command the artillery. Officers subsequently interviewed employers to induce them to keep open the places of any men who joined the defence force and temporarily left their jobs. By 16 April, Worcester had found a full compliment of officers and 130 men had been attested for the two companies of infantry, with 85 for the battery of artillery. Bromsgrove, Evesham and Redditch had raised one company each and special armlets were being issued to all men wearing 'plain clothes'. By this date there had also been a parade of a considerable force on the drill ground at Silver Street, and while most of the local men were staying in their homes, both the public hall in the Cornmarket and the empty factory at Blackpole were made available as billets. Lady Hindlip appealed for magazines, books, papers, games and footballs for the use of the men at Blackpole.[8] Given that unemployment was rising rapidly and had reached 1,615,000 by April 1921, and that food supplies were still short after the wartime restrictions, it is small wonder that men readily enrolled in the new force, if only to receive some pay and to be fed!

On 21 April it was reported that the Blackpole factory had become the Brigade Headquarters for the 48th (South Midland) Brigade; this Special Defence Force comprised men drawn from the whole of Worcestershire and part of Gloucestershire, and was under the command of General Sir H.B. Walker. It was emphasised that the force was not a substitute for the police, but to protect those who wanted to work from those agitators who wished to prevent them from doing so, and to protect life and property. Although the establishment was not yet complete, the brigade now comprised four battalions of infantry, a battery of artillery, a horse and supply column, together with signals and a field ambulance, but as yet no engineers. These 7th and 8th Volunteer Battalions of the Worcestershire Regiment had by this time expanded to 600 and 300 men respectively, and the 4th and 6th Battalions of the Gloucestershire Regiment, 300 and 260 respectively. The artillery was reported to be one battery of 18 pounder guns each from the 66th (Gloucestershire) Royal Field Artillery Brigade and the 67th (Worcestershire) RFA Brigade, as well as a 4.5 howitzer from the 68th (Warwickshire) Brigade. The day before the Brigade HQ was finally assembled, Lord Coventry inspected a parade of 1,200 troops who had arrived at Blackpole.

Colonel R.T. Hillyard now commanded the Headquarters and Captain W. Kirkham was appointed the Camp Adjutant. The feeding arrangements were provided by the Army and Navy Canteen Board. It was reported that the troops were comfortably housed in the workshops at Blackpole, but photographs indicate a different picture – men sleeping on the concrete floors of the bullet shop could not have been comfortable by any means.

Figs. 3.2 and 3.3 Two images of the 90–day volunteer force inside the Blackpole factory which had become the temporary 48th (South Midland) Brigade headquarters, showing the storage of equipment and bedding along the sides of the former production bays. The munitions making machines have by this time gone into storage, but the rows of hold down bolts for them can still be seen in the concrete floor and, more clearly, the retention of the overhead pulley system, which would be reused in the Second World War. In the top photograph, a number of men in uniform are wearing the cap badge of the Gloucestershire Regiment, while another displays the Royal Artillery badge, and yet another in civilian clothing is wearing a volunteer's armband. Both Short Magazine Lee Enfield and Long Lee Enfield rifles can be seen in the lower photograph, leaned against the steel stanchions. (Courtesy of the Cadbury Archive, Mondelez International)

With a large contingent of troops billeted on the edge of Worcester, it is perhaps not surprising that there would be drink-induced trouble in the city centre. It was not long in coming, for on 23 April it was reported that Police Sergeant Miller had arrested Hector Horace McDonald of Bristol for using bad language and breaking a tram window. Inspector Bye of the Tramway Company was of the opinion that he had had too much to drink, whilst the Magistrates Clerk commented that 'it was not a very nice way of starting if you had come here to defend the people'. The magistrates fined McDonald 10 shillings for using bad language, 10 shillings for breaking a tram window and over £3 for court expenses. In default, he was to serve a month in prison. McDonald said that he would pay the fines if given time and this was granted.[9]

This temporary volunteer defence force was not part of the Territorial Force, although the nomenclature may be the same, and many serving Territorials did join it. It contained many old soldiers, including men who had seen service in the recent war. The government announced that it had no intention of keeping the force in being for any period beyond what was absolutely necessary, and that it would be discharged after a return to work by the miners.[10]

In the event the miners' strike was quickly over and the volunteers were released from duty.[11]

Fig. 3.4 This photograph shows a few of the Special Defence Force volunteers who were billeted at Blackpole. Some may have been members of the Territorial Force as two are sporting badges of the Worcestershire Regiment and many wear ribbons of First World War decorations indicating that they have been in the army, and if so would afterwards return to their 'weekend soldiering' at their local drill hall. Does anyone recognise them?
(© Mercian Regiment Museum, reproduced with permission)

Cadbury brothers buy the factory

A large fire occurred at the Cadbury's chocolate factory in Bournville in December 1919 which caused considerable damage and resulted in a need for additional factory space while rebuilding work was carried out. Although it was 22 miles from Bournville, the now redundant No.3 Cartridge Factory with its good communications back to Bournville was available and on 4 August 1921 the factory was conveyed to Cadbury Brothers for a figure of £127,000. The government paid 5% of this sale price to the Kings Norton Metal Company in accordance with their original agreement. The sale included the narrow gauge railway system within the site and allowed for the government to retain two buildings, Numbers 11 and 55 of 3,000 and 12,000 square feet respectively, for the storage of machinery previously used for the production of ammunition. Machinery owned by the government at munitions factories elsewhere was later brought to the site for storage. A key condition of the sale of the site was that any alterations to the property would require the government's consent, presumably to ensure that the site could readily be requisitioned for reuse as a munitions factory.[12]

Fig. 3.5 This oblique aerial view of the Blackpole site when occupied by Cadbury's shows a number of additional features introduced by the company, including increased canal wharfage, playing fields and the estate of staff bungalows in the background. The three small buildings adjoining the bungalows have earth bunds around them and are thought to be the former cartridge filling shops. The two long railway platforms of Blackpole Halt show up as two light-coloured strips on either side of the main railway line, and the tall chimney adjoins the steam boiler room which provided heating for the buildings on the site. The photograph clearly shows the rural setting of the factory during the inter-war period and that Blackpole Lane, later Blackpole Road, was very much a country road.
(Courtesy of the Cadbury Archive, Mondelez International)

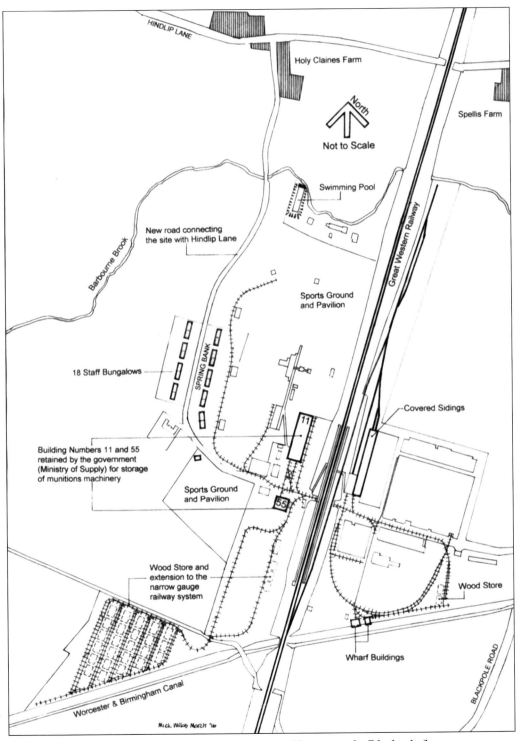

*Fig. 3.6 A plan showing the inter-war additions to the Blackpole factory
made by the Cadbury Company*

Initially, the Cadbury company moved their timber yard and saw mills to Blackpole, the timber being transported by barge from Avonmouth up the River Severn and the Birmingham and Worcester Canal to the site. Much of this timber was stored out-of-doors on the west side of the railway and adjoining the canal, consent being given in 1922 to extend the narrow gauge railway system to this area (see Fig. 3.6) By this date Cadbury's was employing 450 people at the site. The former bullet shop was utilised for the saw mill machinery which had been moved from Bournville, and also provided a dry store for some of the timber prior to its being used to construct chocolate boxes. Within a year the company had also transferred their tin plate store and tin stamping production facilities to the bullet shop. This was quickly followed by the location of their nut store at the site. By 1930 the demand for timber had decreased significantly due to a decline in the use of wooden chocolate boxes and packing cases. Consequently, the company then used the Blackpole site largely as a huge storage facility, including for their cocoa beans, but also moved their marzipan production and the manufacture of cardboard boxes to the factory.[13]

Soon after occupying the Blackpole site, Cadbury's purchased another 76 acres

Fig. 3.7 Mr A. Birchley was employed as a police officer by the Ministry of Munitions at Blackpole during the First World War. He was to become one of the first employees of Cadbury Brothers when the company took over the factory, becoming a caretaker.
(Courtesy of the Cadbury Archive, Mondelez International)

of land on the north side of Barbourne Brook for £3,500 which gave the company access to Hindlip Lane. Part of this extra land was laid out as playing fields, while in 1938 some 12 acres on the south side were sold to Worcester City Council to provide an extension to Perdiswell airfield. In 1924 the company constructed 18 bungalows on the west side of the site for the foreman and maintenance staff. The company provided canteen facilities, while cricket, bowls and tennis were catered for on the sports field, and an open air swimming pool was also constructed (see Fig. 3.6).[14]

As a result of Cadbury's improvements to the site, in 1926 *Berrow's Worcester News* described the Blackpole factory as almost a little township, standing on its own about two miles from Worcester and within easy distance of the Birmingham to Bristol road. The reporter described taking a walk up to Blackpole where he was impressed by the huge piles of timber. He described the buildings as being tastefully arranged, there being pleasant gardens, broad walks and fine playing fields providing accommodation for football, tennis and bowls. Apparently the cricket team wore chocolate coloured caps and the footballers a similar coloured strip. A fine fire station is described, together with the latest model of fire engine and a staff of capable firemen who knew their job.[15]

Immediately after the Second World War, the *Worcester Evening News and Times* thought that it was true to say that the many thousands employed on vital war work had benefited considerably from the improvements that the Cadbury brothers had made in the pre-war days.[16]

During the 19-year occupation of the site between the wars, Cadbury's used the Blackpole factory as only a subsidiary of Bournville, allowing some of the unused buildings to fall into disrepair. Some of the temporary wooden buildings where cartridge filling had taken place simply decayed away. The construction of the bungalows within the danger zone of the previous explosives stores meant that, should the factory return to producing ammunition, either magazines would have to be provided elsewhere or the bungalows evacuated.[17] This being the case, it is surprising that the construction of the bungalows had been allowed by the government.

The rise in Nazism in the 1930s, and the prospect of another war with Germany, gave the government cause to consider again the use of Blackpole for munitions manufacture. Visits were made by government officials in 1933 and 1934 to collect information on what additional plant might be needed, and plans and layouts were drawn up at the drawing office at Woolwich. At the time Blackpole was considered to be no more than a 'reserve small arms ammunition factory'.

Fig. 3.8 Cadbury employees working on large baulks of imported timber in the saw mill at Blackpole, here occupying part of the former bullet shop. The timber would be sawn down to provide the thin wood panels needed for the manufacture of chocolate boxes. Note that the overhead pulley system of the former munitions factory has been removed by this time, presumably to storage in Buildings 11 and 55 elsewhere on the site.
(Courtesy of the Cadbury Archive, Mondelez International)

Fig. 3.9 Another Cadbury inter-war photograph, this showing the substantial scale of just one of the timber stacks at Blackpole. This one is immediately to the west of the railway embankment, with the staff bungalows clearly showing in the background. Buildings 11 and 55 retained by the government for storage purposes can be seen beyond and to the left of the signal box. (Courtesy of the Cadbury Archive, Mondelez International)

Fig. 3.10 This photograph illustrates the use by Cadbury employees of the covered standard gauge railway sidings on the Blackpole site to despatch goods during the inter-war period. (Courtesy of the Cadbury Archive, Mondelez International)

Fig. 3.11 One half of a pair of the semi-detached bungalows on the small estate on the west side of the Blackpole site, built by Cadbury's in 1924 as staff accommodation. While the now mature hedges and trees prevent an extensive view of this site, the quality of the housing is clear and reflects the caring attitude of this company towards its employees. (Photo by Mick Wilks, August 2015)

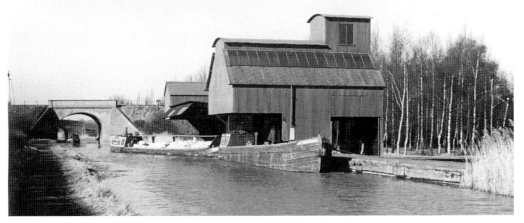

Fig. 3.12 The improved wharfage created by Cadbury's alongside the canal at Blackpole can be seen in this inter-war photograph. The narrowboat, which has probably come up the River Severn and the Birmingham to Worcester Canal, from Gloucester Docks, appears to have a cargo of timber to be used in the manufacture of chocolate boxes. (Courtesy of the Cadbury Archive, Mondelez International)

Fig. 3.13 The same scene photographed in 2010 with the main building still overhanging the canal, but now re-roofed with a lower ridgeline. (Photo by Mick Wilks)

4   BLACKPOLE IN THE SECOND WORLD WAR

The government takes back Blackpole Factory, eventually

The Cadbury company asked a number of times during 1939 whether the factory would be requisitioned for a return to cartridge manufacturing use, but received no firm reply one way or another. Cadbury's appear to have been left in ignorance about the government's thoughts for the factory and so filled their buildings at Blackpole to capacity with cocoa beans and tin plate. Much time and money would consequently be lost by the company when the government finally decided to requisition the factory.

For six years from 1934 the factory at Blackpole had in fact been under consideration by the government for a return to ammunition production. Their storage facilities on the site were still filled with machinery dating back to the First World War, but the return of small arms ammunition production to Blackpole was reckoned to require many of these machines to be scrapped, removed to storage space elsewhere or modernised to suit up-to-date processes. The buildings themselves would need to be adapted to accommodate new designs of machines and techniques of manufacture, while cartridge filling would need new buildings to be erected. Much time was subsequently wasted by officials looking for an alternative site. In 1934 some of the machines stored at Blackpole were fitted with automatic feeding devices, but little else was done until the spring of 1937, when a proposal was considered to spend £140,000 on reconditioning the factory for the production of 8,000,000 rounds of ammunition a week, while Woolwich would produce 11,000,000 rounds.[1] One cause of delay in returning production to Blackpole was the development of multi-punch machines which would replace the older single-punch machines and required considerably less factory floorspace. During this period of indecision, some of the older cartridge-making machines stored at Blackpole, together with the newer machines, were moved to Royal Ordnance Factories at Radway Green (Cheshire) and Swynnerton (near Stoke on Trent), only for the machines to be moved back again to Blackpole when a decision was finally made to requisition the site.

During 1939 Blackpole was finally earmarked by the government as Small Arms Ammunition Factory No.5 (SAAF No.5) to be run on an agency basis. The costs to bring the factory back into production were estimated to be £319,000, made up of £90,000 on refurbishing the buildings, £67,000 on internal services, £103,000 on plant, £24,000 on equipment and tools, £20,000 on external services and £15,000 on passive air defence and camouflage (these were unspecified but the provision of air raid shelters, painting the outside of the factory in camouflage colours and making blackout arrangements would seem likely).[2]

The appointment of Winston Churchill as Prime Minister on 10 May 1940 and the establishment of a coalition government, brought a change of pace and vigour to Britain's defence policy. On 22 May the Emergency Powers Act passed through parliament and received Royal Assent, just before the evacuation of the British Expeditionary Force from Dunkirk started. This legislation gave the government wide-ranging powers over the use of land, buildings and people in much the same way as DORA had in the First World War. Cadbury's received notification on 17 June that the government would be taking over their factory and that some of their employees might be taken on. By July 1940 and the start of the Battle of Britain, the shortage of small arms ammunition manufacturing sites had become acute and the site at Blackpole was finally repossessed by the government in two stages: 34½ acres including the factory and recreation grounds on 14 July, and 28½ acres comprising the bungalows and some pasture land on 31 August.

It was agreed at a meeting at Worcester between the government's chief valuer, the district valuer and representatives of Cadbury's that compensation of £8,500 per annum would be paid to the company for the occupation of the main factory and grounds, and £475 per annum for use of the bungalows and pasture land. Compensation was also paid to Cadbury's for the work entailed in removing their stored materials back to Bournville. In May 1941 Cadbury's offered to sell the Blackpole site back to the government at a price of £155,202, but the government's valuer considered that the market value of the site and buildings in the state they were in when requisitioned was only £132,000. A decision to purchase the site was therefore deferred and, since it was not necessary to keep the factory in production after the war, subsequently not proceeded with.[3]

Production recommences at Blackpole
Initially it was decided that the Blackpole factory would be used only for limited small arms ammunition component manufacture and would be managed on an agency basis by the Metal Division of Imperial Chemical Industries (ICI). In July 1940 the tool room was prepared and some machine tools, received from America, made ready. With the intention of keeping a number of Cadbury's' workforce together, work suitable for semi-skilled people was transferred from the ICI Works at Witton, Birmingham, and the training of tool makers begun. The preparation of the plant and installation of tool making facilities was well advanced by September 1940, with about 30 workers and a number of management staff on site, when circumstances changed dramatically. Woolwich Arsenal was heavily bombed on 7 September and again on 3 October and as a consequence the Ministry of Supply decided to use Blackpole as an additional Royal Ordnance Factory (ROF) and to transfer equipment from Woolwich. Blackpole was subsequently designated ROF No.20.

Coincidentally, some of the carpet manufacturers at Kidderminster had approached the Ministry of Supply offering their then vacant factories for government use, and a scheme to accommodate small arms ammunition production was discussed on

9 October at the offices of Brintons, attended by representatives of the Ministry of Supply and Woolwich Arsenal. Component manufacture by ICI under the SAAF No.5 scheme, originally planned for Blackpole, was subsequently accommodated in three requisitioned carpet factories in Kidderminster, namely Brintons, which made the tooling required, Tomkinson's, which manufactured the bullets and Carpet Trades, which manufactured the cartridges. The propellant filling and assembly was completed at the ICI establishment at Summerfield, on the southern approaches to Kidderminster. Between 4,000 and 5,000 people were engaged in small arms ammunition manufacture at Kidderminster.[4]

The announcement that alternative accommodation for some of the Woolwich plant was needed had come on 18 September and on the following day Woolwich engineers arrived at Blackpole to make preparations for its installation. However, with only 25% of the equipment installed, production of components for .303 tracer ammunition began at Blackpole in October, with the majority of the cartridge filling being carried

out at Swynnerton, the remainder at Woolwich. The transfer of equipment from Woolwich for producing .303 ammunition at Blackpole was completed in November and by the end of the year a substantial, but unspecified, output was being achieved. Alterations and improvements to the buildings continued until December 1941.[5]

In the summer of 1941 it was decided to increase the production of 9mm ammunition components and reduce the production of .303 rounds. Consequently, some of the equipment at Blackpole was converted to produce 9mm calibre ammunition for the soon to be introduced Sten Machine Carbine. Production of cartridges for 9mm rounds was begun in November 1941.[6]

Production figures for small arms ammunition produced at Blackpole in the Second World War are difficult to find, but from April to June 1943, for which information is recorded, they were:

Fig. 4.1 These two women munitions workers at Blackpole are placing lead-filled cupro-nickel .303 calibre projectiles or bullets in stackable wooden trays, presumably for transportation to Swynnerton, where they would be pressed into 'filled' cartridge casings to complete the process of manufacturing finished cartridges. The crowded floorspace behind provides just a small indication of the high proportion of women working at Blackpole in the Second World War. (© Imperial War Museum, image no: L309)

April   12,860,000 rounds of .303 tracer and 1,890,000 rounds of 9mm.

May   11,740,000 rounds of .303 tracer and 830,000 of 9mm.

June   10,600,000 rounds of .303 tracer and 760,000 rounds of 9mm.[7]

Presumably production was dropping as it increased at other factories.

Working at the factory during the above period was James Cassidy, a native of Eltham in Kent but then living in the Astwood area of Worcester. He was a veteran of both the Boer and the First World Wars and was living in retirement when the Second World War started. He returned to the world of work at Blackpole where he became a check gauger on the night shift, checking the dimensions of manufactured components accurately by means of a gauge and so testing the efficiency and accuracy of the manufacturing machines and their operators. He was chosen, by both the management and the employees, to receive the British Empire Medal (Civil Division) as a representative of the workers of the factory for achieving their level of production. The investiture took place at Buckingham Palace on 16 March 1943.[8]

The workforce at Blackpole

Although incomplete, figures for the initial growth and then decline of the workforce engaged on cartridge manufacture at Blackpole from 1940 to 1945 are set out in the Appendix. Production started at Blackpole with a nucleus of men who moved from Woolwich Royal Ordnance Factory. It was planned that women would be employed in significant numbers and of an eventual target figure of 4,000 employees, 3,100 were to have been women. The target figure was never quite reached, with the peak number of employees being recorded in December 1942 as 3,936. Reasons for the dwindling numbers of employees from 1943 onwards are not recorded, a reduction that is surprising since the demand for small arms ammunition would be expected to rise as the expansion of the armed forces continued, certainly until D-Day in June 1944 and the subsequent campaign in North-West Europe. In March 1943 a number of 'mobile' workers from Hereford (presumably from the shell filling Royal Ordnance Factory at Rotherwas) were transferred to Blackpole. The workforce gradually declined to 207 employees in

Fig. 4.2 A happy group of Second World War munitions workers from Blackpole, with at least three Royal Navy sailors, somewhere in Worcester (possibly overlooking Pitchcroft race course). Nearest the camera is Mrs Annie Bilby; none of the others have been identified. (Courtesy of Doreen Stevenson, daughter of Mrs Bilby)

June 1945, of whom 25 were women, when the manager of the works is recorded as being a Mr Hunt and the superintendent a Mr Hood.[9]

A proportion of the women working at Blackpole were conscripted following the passing of the National Service (No.2) Act in December 1941 to deal with a national labour shortage. Under this legislation, single women between the ages of 20 (reduced to 19 in 1943) and 30 would be offered a choice of joining the auxiliary services (Auxiliary Territorial Service, Women's Auxiliary Air Force or Women's Royal Naval Service), the Civil Defence or industry. If they chose the latter they would be directed to a specific factory. Initially, the women worked a three eight-hour shift system at Blackpole, with the men working two twelve-hour shifts. This limited the amount of overtime women could work and they worked an average of 43 hours a week. From 5 December 1943 the system was changed to two shifts for both men and women, the average weekly hours per week for a women consequently rising to nearly 50 hours. (Some of the memories of women who worked in the factory noted below suggest that there was a move back to a three shift system, but this is not confirmed by documentary sources.)

Average weekly wages for the women rose from £3 17s 4d in July 1943 to £4 2s 6d in January 1944.[10]

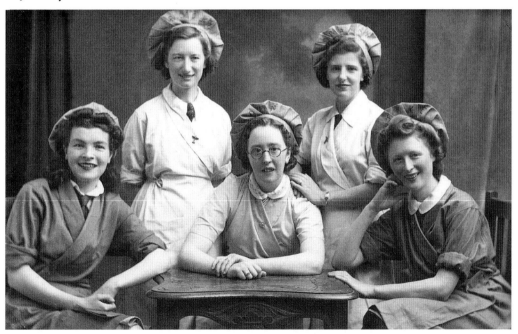

Fig. 4.3 Another group of happy Blackpole munitionettes in the Second World War. Note that they no longer wear the loose smocks of their First World War equivalents, but much smarter overalls, and the headgear, known as a 'snood', is a much larger affair. The two at the back of the photograph are wearing miniature brass Spitfire brooches, an indication that they have contributed to the local Spitfire Fund. From left to right are Kathleen Bourne, Olive Miles, a charge hand known as 'Lil', Mary Bransfield and Joan Turner. (Courtesy of Joan Jacobs, née Turner)

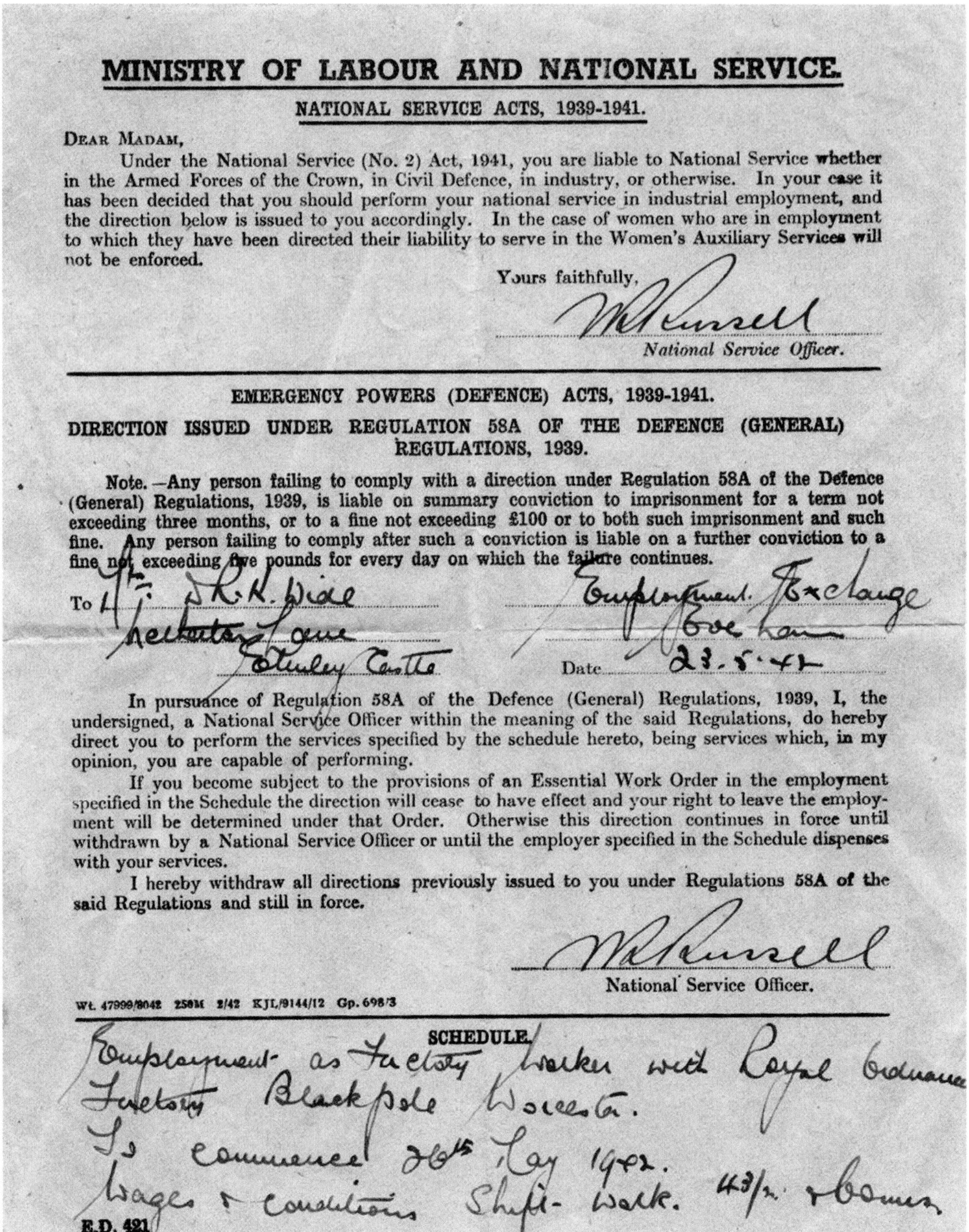

MINISTRY OF LABOUR AND NATIONAL SERVICE.

NATIONAL SERVICE ACTS, 1939-1941.

DEAR MADAM,

    Under the National Service (No. 2) Act, 1941, you are liable to National Service whether in the Armed Forces of the Crown, in Civil Defence, in industry, or otherwise. In your case it has been decided that you should perform your national service in industrial employment, and the direction below is issued to you accordingly. In the case of women who are in employment to which they have been directed their liability to serve in the Women's Auxiliary Services will not be enforced.

Yours faithfully,

[signature] WK Russell

National Service Officer.

EMERGENCY POWERS (DEFENCE) ACTS, 1939-1941.

DIRECTION ISSUED UNDER REGULATION 58A OF THE DEFENCE (GENERAL) REGULATIONS, 1939.

    Note.—Any person failing to comply with a direction under Regulation 58A of the Defence (General) Regulations, 1939, is liable on summary conviction to imprisonment for a term not exceeding three months, or to a fine not exceeding £100 or to both such imprisonment and such fine. Any person failing to comply after such a conviction is liable on a further conviction to a fine not exceeding five pounds for every day on which the failure continues.

To *[handwritten] Mi̇ss D.R.K. Wide, Rectory Lane, Elmley Castle*   *Employment Exchange Evesham*

    Date *[handwritten] 23.5.42*

    In pursuance of Regulation 58A of the Defence (General) Regulations, 1939, I, the undersigned, a National Service Officer within the meaning of the said Regulations, do hereby direct you to perform the services specified by the schedule hereto, being services which, in my opinion, you are capable of performing.

    If you become subject to the provisions of an Essential Work Order in the employment specified in the Schedule the direction will cease to have effect and your right to leave the employment will be determined under that Order. Otherwise this direction continues in force until withdrawn by a National Service Officer or until the employer specified in the Schedule dispenses with your services.

    I hereby withdraw all directions previously issued to you under Regulations 58A of the said Regulations and still in force.

[signature] WK Russell

National Service Officer.

Wt. 47999/8042 258M 2/42 KJL/9144/12 Gp. 698/3

SCHEDULE

[handwritten] Employment as Factory worker with Royal Ordnance Factory Blackpole Worcester. To commence 26th May 1942. Wages & conditions Shift work. 43/1. + bonus

E.D. 421

Fig. 4.4 Women directed to the Services or industry received this standard letter from the Ministry of Labour and National Service. This particular one was sent to Daisy Wide of Elmley Castle directing her to work at the Royal Ordnance Factory at Blackpole in May 1942, but not before she had undertaken a medical examination (see above right).
(Courtesy of Daisy Wide)

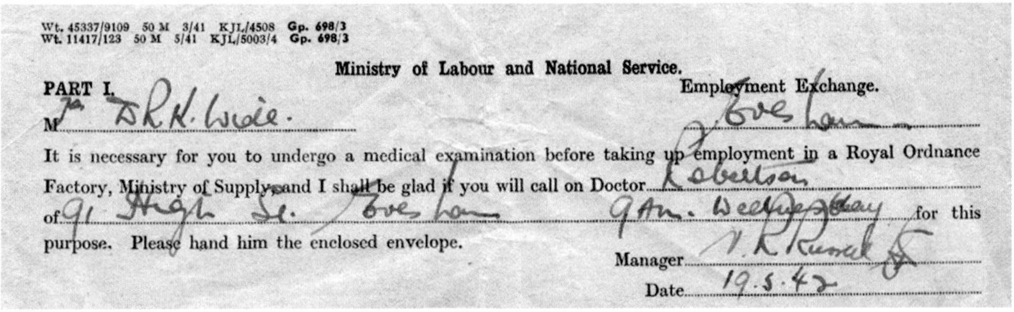

Wt. 45337/9109 50 M 3/41 KJL/4508 Gp. 698/3
Wt. 11417/123 50 M 5/41 KJL/5003/4 Gp. 698/3

Ministry of Labour and National Service.

PART I.   Employment Exchange.

M~~rs~~ *D.R.K. Wide.*   *Evesham*

It is necessary for you to undergo a medical examination before taking up employment in a Royal Ordnance

Factory, Ministry of Supply, and I shall be glad if you will call on Doctor *Robertson*

of *91 High St. Evesham*   *9 A.m. Wednesday*   for this

purpose. Please hand him the enclosed envelope.

Manager *N.R. Russell*

Date *19.5.42*

Fig. 4.5 *The 'request' sent to Daisy Wide to undergo a medical examination before she could
start work at the Blackpole factory. (Courtesy of Daisy Wide)*

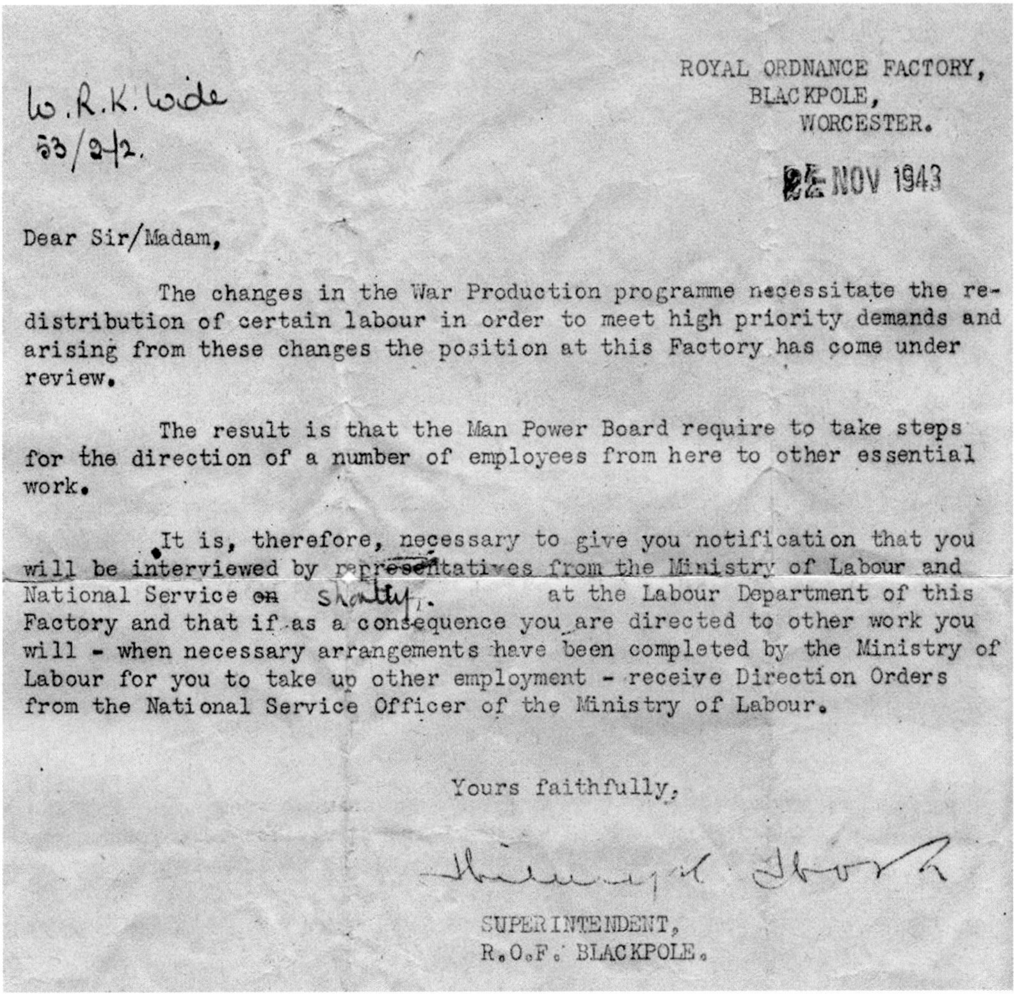

W.R.K. Wide
53/2/2.

ROYAL ORDNANCE FACTORY,
BLACKPOLE,
WORCESTER.

22 NOV 1943

Dear Sir/Madam,

        The changes in the War Production programme necessitate the re-
distribution of certain labour in order to meet high priority demands and
arising from these changes the position at this Factory has come under
review.

        The result is that the Man Power Board require to take steps
for the direction of a number of employees from here to other essential
work.

        It is, therefore, necessary to give you notification that you
will be interviewed by representatives from the Ministry of Labour and
National Service on Shortly,   at the Labour Department of this
Factory and that if as a consequence you are directed to other work you
will - when necessary arrangements have been completed by the Ministry of
Labour for you to take up other employment - receive Direction Orders
from the National Service Officer of the Ministry of Labour.

                    Yours faithfully,

                    SUPERINTENDENT,
                    R.O.F. BLACKPOLE.

Fig. 4.6 *The letter sent to Daisy Wide warning her that she was to be 'redirected'.
In fact she moved to the Morganite Crucible Works at Norton, later leaving for health reasons.
(Courtesy of Daisy Wide)*

Margaret McKerron was living in Aberdeen when, in about 1942 and aged 21, she was directed to work at the Blackpole factory. Apparently she was upset at being sent so far away from home to work. She was billeted with four other girls with a Mrs Collett at 33 Sansome Walk, who was not particularly welcoming, having been obliged presumably to take in the lodgers. Margaret has not left any record of her time at Blackpole, so it is not possible to say what type of work she undertook, but her son has inherited a number of photographs and other mementoes from the time. Margaret left Blackpole in April 1945 to get married, and returned to Scotland.[11]

Figs. 4.7 and 4.8 Margaret McKerron, second from the right in the top photograph and on the left in the lower photograph, with four of her fellow Blackpole munitions workers, presumably those with whom she was billeted. (Courtesy of Bryan Massie, son of Margaret Massie, née McKerron)

Fig. 4.9 33 Sansome Walk, Worcester, the wartime billet of Margaret McKerron and her four friends from the Blackpole factory. (Photo by Mick Wilks)

Memories of some of the women employees at the factory

Mrs Mary Addison (née Young) had previously been in service when she was directed at the age of 18 to work at the Blackpole factory in 1942. She remained at the factory until the end of the war. During that time she lived at Malvern Wells, from where she would take the train to the halt at Blackpole. Initially she recalls working on the two-shift system, and that later this became the three-shift system. She worked in the Brown Room where, wearing brown overalls, she was involved in trimming 9mm bullets, although occasionally she would be moved onto other work, depending on what was required at the time.

Mrs D. Bowen (née Mills) also started work at Blackpole in 1942 and made cartridge cases on a punch machine. She left in 1945 to go to Baggots, where she operated a lathe, and then to Kays assembling steam irons.

Mrs Kathleen Brewer (née Wright) was another conscript, who at the age of 19 went to work at Blackpole. Having married in 1943, she left the factory in 1944 to have a child. Until she was 21, Kathleen had worked in the wages office, but from 1942 to 1944 she moved into one of the examination rooms, checking both bullets and cartridge cases. She recalls that the bullets were manufactured at Blackpole and had to be individually weighed when examined.

Mrs Ida Cale (née Phillips) volunteered to work at the Blackpole factory in 1942, just as she turned 18 and so before she was conscripted. Prior to working at Blackpole she had been in service. She left the factory at the end of the war when she was made redundant. While at Blackpole, she worked in the Brown Room and her task was to push .303 calibre cartridge cases into two machines which trimmed them to size, initially working an a two-shift system and later a three-shift regime. She recalls that 9mm calibre bullets were made in the Green Room and that the Blue Room was where the cartridges were checked. She recalls that there were entertainments on occasions in the staff canteen.

Fig. 4.10 An ROF sew-on badge issued to Margaret McKerron (see opposite), but apparently never worn on her overalls. (Courtesy of Brian Massie)

Mrs Joan Jacobs (née Turner) went to work at Blackpole in 1941, after being conscripted. Prior to this she had worked as a nanny. She married in 1943 and left the factory in 1944 to have a child. Joan lived at Droitwich and travelled each day by train to the Blackpole Halt, where she recalls having been issued with a badge in order to get into the works. She found the change of employment from nanny to factory work to be quite a shock. Her work initially entailed packing tracer bullets into cases, then she was moved to a machine used for trimming bullets of .303 calibre and tracer. This machine required her to stand for the whole shift, and there were 12 such machines in a row. A Mr Davies was in charge. Initially she worked the two-shift system, but later on the three-shift system. She recalls that there were many Irish girls working at the factory and that they lived at a hostel off Blackpole Road. She also recalls some of the men at the factory going on strike, and the women pelting them with bullet cases.

Mrs Doris Monk (née Rouse) began work at the Blackpole factory in June 1943. Initially, she worked in the office as a typist, which had been her previous occupation. Subsequently she was moved to an examination room where she and her colleagues checked the quality of both bullets and cartridges, and of both .303 and 9mm calibres. There she did shift work, alternating 14 days of day shifts with 14 of night work. She recalls that the day shift was from 7am to 5pm, Mondays to Fridays, and from 7am to 11am on Saturdays. Night shifts were from 9pm to 7am. She remembers that where the cartridges were made, the workers were on three shift days, with the hours 7am to 3pm, 3pm to 10pm and 10pm to 7am. Both cartridges and bullets were sent to Swynnerton for filling with propellant and assembly. She returned to office and typing work in May 1944, and left the factory two weeks before the war ended. Whilst working at Blackpole, Doris lived with her mother in Holly Mount Road, Worcester, and would catch a bus which meant leaving home at 6.15am to arrive at the factory in time for the morning shift, the bus having been all round the estates in Worcester. Her mother had worked at the Blackpole factory as a munitionette during the First World War and had two of the factory workers billeted at her house during the Second World War. The first two girls came from Nottingham and when one of them left, her replacement came from the north of Scotland. Doris recalls that other girls working at Blackpole came from Durham and Kent. Her other memories include there being no heating in the factory, (though this conflicts with the memories of Clifford Lord, noted below) and of entertainments in the canteen on some lunchtimes.

Peggy Rann (née Law) recalls, as a 19-year-old then living in Burgess Hill in Sussex, volunteering with her friend Margaret to join the Land Army in 1942. Being November, the recruiting officer suggested that they could be sent temporarily to a munitions factory in Worcester and then transfer to the Land Army in the following spring. The planned transfer to the Land Army failed to occur and she and Margaret remained at the Blackpole factory until 1945. Their accommodation was at the Malvern Hall Hostel off Blackpole Road (see below), with girls who came from all over Britain. With three-shift working at the factory (which she recalls were from 6am to 2pm for the morning shift, 2pm to 11pm for the afternoon shift, and 11pm to 6am for the night shift) she had to get used to sleeping at the hostel during the daylight hours. Her particular part of the factory was filled with rows and rows of little machines, rather like slot machines, alongside which were large boxes of bullets. A handful of these (five or six) would be put down a small chute, after which a handle was pulled and the bullets would travel around the machine, before dropping into a box. From this description it is difficult to determine what this process was, but it could have been trimming the bullets to length. After working a shift, the girls would rush back to the hostel to see what post might have arrived for them.[12]

After being evacuated from Kent, Mrs Kathleen Smith (née Driver) worked at a school in Malvern Wells. On being conscripted she was informed that she would have to work at either the Worcester Royal Porcelain factory, which was then doing war work, or at the Blackpole munitions factory. She chose the latter and started work, she thought, in about 1942. She continued living in Malvern Wells and travelled to Blackpole by train. Her travelling companion was a Mrs Addison, although she was then unmarried and had the maiden-name of Young. Kathleen worked on a machine that made bullet cases, both of .303 and 9mm calibres. This was located in the so-called Brown Room where everyone wore brown overalls and the bonnets known as snoods. From the Brown Room, the bullets were tipped into small trucks which were pushed around on the narrow gauge railway lines within the site. She recalls working initially on 12-hour shifts, which were 7am to 7pm and then 7pm to 7am. This later changed to a three eight-hour shift system starting at 7am, 3pm and 10pm. She too remembers occasional entertainments at lunchtimes in the canteen, and that the popular radio programme, 'Workers Playtime' was constantly broadcast on loudspeakers throughout the factory.

Mrs Daisy Wide and her sister, Miss May Oakley were both conscripted to work at the Blackpole factory. Daisy started work at Blackpole on 26 May 1942, then went to work at the Morganite Crucible Works at Norton, but left in November 1943 for health reasons. She then worked on various market gardens, but was not a member of the Women's Land Army. Both of the sisters worked in the Blue Room and wore blue uniforms. This was an examination room where 9mm calibre bullets were checked, and they both worked the three-shift system. Living in Elmley Castle, the two sisters cycled to the main Pershore to Evesham Road, where they would catch one of the works buses to take them to Blackpole.

Women in many occupations did sterling work during both world wars and the recently erected memorial in Whitehall pays tribute to this (Fig. 5.7). In addition, Coventry's old cathedral, ruined in the bombing of November 1940, incorporates a memorial to all those who served on the Home Front. The possibility of rewarding former Home Front workers on an individual basis was mooted by the late author, but in a reply of 28 August 2009, the government's Department of Business Innovation and Skills, while recognising the service of women in the wars, considered that it would now be difficult to identify those involved in the armaments industry at the time. Additionally, they pointed out that many of the firms no longer exist and consequently there would not be records of those employed and so the claims could not be verified. As a result it was considered impractical to recognise the contribution of women workers on an individual basis.

Maintaining the factory
Clifford Lord began his time at Blackpole factory in 1942 as an apprentice in the Maintenance and Engineering Department (MED). The MED team were accommodated in a small square building on the south side of the main production building, close to the railway. There he worked under the direction of Jock Kelly who was, in Clifford's opinion, 'the best engineer in the factory', but a bit of a bully towards the apprentices. Each engineer had a fitter, a labourer and an apprentice working for him, many of the labourers apparently being Irish. At the time Clifford started, the working hours were

based on two 12-hour shifts for the men, and three eight-hour shifts for the women. This was later changed to three eight-hour shifts for all. He recalls that the factory was producing cartridge cases and bullets, but did not do the filling with propellant. One of the statistics he remembers being told was that it had been calculated that it took, on average, 100 bullets to kill one German, and so the demand for small arms ammunition was very great. (This seems to be an underestimate, since the same statistic for the recent campaign in Afghanistan could be counted in the thousands, and it was considerably more during the First World War.)

Clifford initially travelled to work from his home in Tunnel Hill by bike, which he had bought from Halfords for £3 or so. Bikes were kept in an unlocked shed near the entrance to the factory from where his was stolen, and his journey to work then entailed running down from Tunnel Hill to the Astwood Halt, sited immediately to the north of the Blackpole Road/Brickfields Road junction. This halt was apparently built in 1936 as one of several to facilitate the movement of workers around the city and had open platforms, but there is no sign of it now. From there Clifford would travel on what was locally called the Flying Banana, a GWR AEC Diesel Railcar in the standard GWR livery of brown and cream, paying 3d each way. This service was specifically laid on for Blackpole staff and picked up passengers at each of the stations and halts in Worcester, and was apparently very disruptive to the mainline rail traffic. Clifford recalls being staggeringly tired on the walk back up Tunnel Hill at the end of a 12-hour shift.

In the Second World War the machines used on the production lines were a combination of reused machines which had been stored at Blackpole since the First World

Fig. 4.11 The GWR AEC diesel railcar, once a familiar sight in Worcester when delivering workers to Blackpole Halt. Now only a few remain in railway museums, but this model portrays the unique appearance of the 'Flying Banana'. (Courtesy of John Loynes, modeller par excellence)

War, and more modern machines manufactured by the Cincinatti Company which had been supplied from America under the Lend-Lease scheme. The machinery was largely driven by an overhead pulley and belt system, some of it 30 feet above the shop floor. The maintenance of this system of power drive involved the engineers and apprentices clambering along the steel girders of the roof structure tightrope fashion, with the attendant risks of falling. There was no health and safety risk assessment in those days; the job just had to be done. Maintenance included replacement of the white metal bearings along the drive shafts and of the drive belts themselves. Since payment of the production staff was on a piecework basis, the maintenance staff were under constant pressure from the workforce, as well as the management, to keep the machinery working. Installation of any new overhead shafting and pulley systems would involve drilling the steel roof girders for the bearing housings by hand using a ratchet operated drill, which Clifford recalls as being particularly hard, physically, to operate. The engineers wore composition soled boots for their work, which were standard issue in Royal Ordnance factories.

The technology used in the manufacture of cartridge cases and bullet cases, which were formed from brass and cupro-nickel cups respectively, was by a series of punching processes with the metals in a cold state. The First World War presses used in this process can be recognised in Figure 2.12 as having large flywheels to ensure no loss of momentum during the sequence of punching processes. The overhead belt drive would operate on one of two pulleys, one providing drive for the machine, the other free-running so that the machine could be stopped by the operator moving the driving belt sideways from the drive pulley to the other by means of a lever. The American machines introduced in the Second World War were more complicated and more troublesome than the earlier machines, making the repairs more difficult.

One of the more complex of the production processes was the lead filling of the bullet casings. This involved molten lead being poured into the hoppers of the machines and the use of a 900 ton hydraulic press. The machines produced a stream of solidifying lead which had to be accurately guided into the bullet casings. All of this had to be maintained by the MED Team, whose work also included repairing the glands on the hydraulic pumps and ensuring a constant and plentiful supply of cooling water from tanks in the roof space.

Buster Martin was the foreman of the works, and one of Clifford's memories is of the constant mickey-taking he used to harden up the apprentices.

Another member of the staff was Charlie Dance, the driver of a small steam tank engine that was used to move materials around the site. Jock Kelly, the maintenance engineer to whom Clifford was apprenticed, often worked on the engine, mainly repairing leaking steam pipe joints. This way, Clifford got to know Charlie very well. As part of Clifford's maintenance tasks, he was given responsibility for clearing out the fire grate of the coal-fired heating boiler to ensure that it worked efficiently. This meant getting inside the fire grate while it was still cooling down, but still quite hot, and chipping off the clinker from the fire bars with a hammer and chisel. The chimney shown in some photographs of the Blackpole site is for this boiler (see Figs. 1.2, 2.10 and 2.11), which provided heat for the whole factory.[13]

Trouble at the factory

Unlike during the First World War, when the Blackpole factory remained strike-free, problems were experienced with the skilled engineers during the Second World War. Both Clifford Lord and Joan Jacobs recall that when the management had introduced semi-skilled labour, known as dilutees, to the factory, this caused problems with the skilled men over pay differentials and caused a short-lived strike. The apprentices virtually ran the factory during this period, much to the initial hostility of the girls on the production line, who attacked them using bullet casings as missiles – until they realised that with the machines not working through lack of maintenance they would not receive their full pay, and consequently stopped their attacks.

Housing the workforce

Clifford Lord thought that the majority of the workers were billeted throughout Worcester, and that the most of them walked to work, with about 10% arriving on bikes and 20 or 30% by train or bus from the outlying areas. The local authority had built many houses in the Brickfields area during the 1920s meaning that many of the Blackpole workers were billeted in this area. Consequently, at the shift changes, Blackpole Road would be full of people walking to or from the factory and their billets. He remembers that the road would be full of different accents, including Scottish, Welsh and Geordie, but predominantly Irish.

As well as billeting workers with local families, a site, located to the east of Blackpole Road, was acquired on 6 August 1941 for the construction of a hostel with a planned occupation of 500 (machine) operatives and 69 staff (probably those carrying out administrative and managerial functions). Construction started on 11 August, with a target completion for the end of January 1942 at a cost of £155,500. Originally just designated Hostel No.5, it was later called Malvern Hall Hostel. The living accommodation was in the form of six single-storey H blocks of wooden construction, with a brick-built communal building (see Figs. 4.12 and 4.15). By October 1942 it was 75% occupied, and it continued in use until the 1950s (possibly temporarily housing returning troops and their families in the late 1940s).[14] Initial weekly rental charges for accommodation at the hostel in 1941 was 27 shillings and 6 pence for men and 22 shillings and 6 pence for women, but by 1945 these had reduced to 25 shillings a week for men and 20 shillings for women. These costs included two meals on weekdays and three on Sundays.[15]

Peggy Law (née Rand), recalls that Malvern Hall was in fact the name of the communal building on the west side of the hostel site, but in due time this became the name adopted by the residents for the whole of the hostel. Peggy describes the communal building as being like a single storey hotel, of brick construction and very large. On entering the main door there was a reception area with a long enquiries desk, behind which were pigeon holes where letters and small parcels were kept until collected by the hostel residents. Malvern Hall also accommodated a refreshment room where coffee and biscuits were available, and a small dance hall which it is estimated could probably hold about 200 people, or 100 dancing couples. There were also a couple of lounges, a shop, two kitchens, dining rooms and a table tennis room.

Peggy lived in one of the wooden H-Blocks, hers being opposite the entrance to the communal building, and she recalls that the half-dozen separate blocks were serviced by roads and footpaths. The walk from factory to hostel took about 20 minutes and she remembers that, although Blackpole Road was quite wide, there were no pavements. She describes it as a country road with fields on either side of the hostel. None of the land was wasted between the H-Blocks, this being cultivated and planted with soft fruit bushes, as part of the dig for victory campaign, and to provide food for the hostel. Each arm of the H-Blocks was served by a central corridor, with up to a half-dozen separate rooms on each side of the plain concrete-surfaced corridors. The southern ends of each H-Block were utilised for bathrooms and toilets. Each of the rooms would accommodate two girls, containing two beds, two chests of drawers and two chairs. Peggy shared her room with her friend, Margaret, with two Welsh sisters in the next-door room and a Scottish girl in the room opposite.

Fig. 4.12 A view of part of Malvern Hall Hostel, off Blackpole Road, showing some of the H-Block living quarters, and taken from the roof of the communal building. Mrs Peggy Law, née Rann) lived in the first building on the left, opposite the front entrance to the communal building. Of note are the overhead heating pipes which traversed the site, a game of netball being played in the foreground, and the cultivation of the spaces between the buildings which appear to be planted with soft-fruit bushes, presumably to supply the canteen.
(Courtesy of Peggy Law)

The hostel site was purchased by the Midlands Electricity Board (MEB) in the 1950s and was subsequently largely redeveloped for office use, with a canteen, garaging, storage and workshops, together with associated car parking and recreational facilities. Over the years the original hostel buildings have gradually disappeared until nothing appears to remain to reflect the site's former use.[16] Currently, the MEB buildings are being redeveloped yet again and replaced with residential development.

Clifford Lord and the MED Team were also responsible for the maintenance of the hostel buildings. He recalls that these hostel buildings were initially, and entirely, occupied by women, who created a great community feeling. The majority of the women were young and naïve Irish girls. Unwanted pregnancies were apparently quite commonplace.

In addition to the hostel, an estate of 200 two-storey houses was built on the south side of Tolladine Road for occupation by married workers. The scheme was approved for construction in October 1941.[17] The houses still exist in Teme Road and Avon Road and are of an unusual modernist design, with flat roofs. Designed by Jeffrey Jellicoe, a London architect, this is one of several such estates built in Britain during the war incorporating concrete roofs and floors, with brick infill panels for the walls. The structures largely avoided the use of timber which was then in short supply. The flat concrete roofs were intended to resist the fire of incendiary bombs and one room of the house was reinforced to provide an air raid shelter from the blast effect of high explosive bombs.[18]

Fig. 4.13 These flat-roofed houses, located in the Teme and Avon roads, off Tolladine Road, Worcester, were specifically built in the Second World War for use as staff houses by Blackpole munitions workers with families. (Photo by Colin Jones, 2010)

Fig. 4.14 This close up of a terrace (semi-detached houses were also built) of the flat-roofed houses in the Tolladine area, illustrates the form of the staff houses designed by the architect, Jeffrey Jellicoe, to use a minimum of wood in the structure (a strategic material in the Second World War). Mainly built of reinforced concrete with a brick skin, the houses incorporated a strengthened room to form an air raid shelter, and the flat roof was intended to resist the heat of incendiary bombs. Other examples of this form of Jellicoe housing can be found in all parts of Britain where munitions factories had been operating in the Second World War.
(Photo by Mick Wilks, 2010)

A special bus would drive through the estate at 6.30am to pick up the workers and take them to the factory.

Ken Murton recalled that his father was one of the first munitions workers to move up to Blackpole from London after the Woolwich Arsenal was bombed and lived firstly in the Springbank bungalows built by Cadbury's in the 1920s. He then moved to one of the houses in Teme Road.[19]

Protecting the factory and workforce

From the early 1930s it had become certain that in any future conflict, industry and the civilian population would be the subject of air attack of greater severity than hitherto, and that the use of poison gas could be expected. Numerous pieces of legislation were passed by the government during the period leading up the Second World War to establish an Air Raid Precautions organisation and prepare the country for air attack. As in the First World War, the responsibility for implementing the government's policy was delegated to local authorities, and it was the Munich crisis in 1938 that gave impetus to the practical provision of facilities to meet the expected intense air attack.

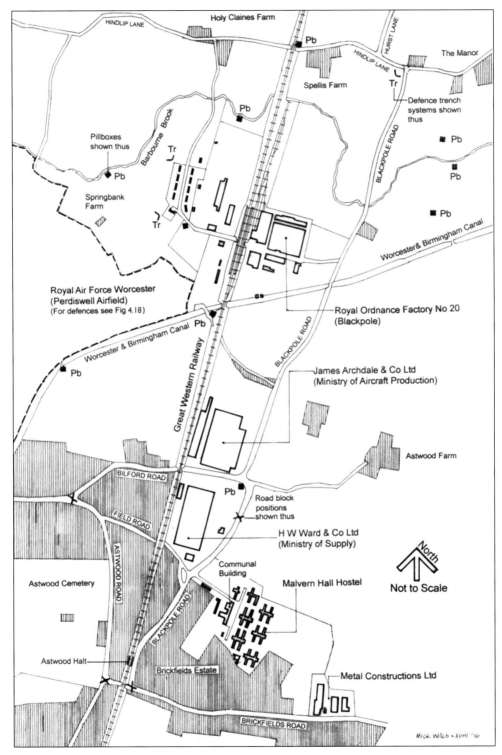

Fig. 4.15 Blackpole and area in the Second World War

Warning of an imminent attack would be given by sirens, the warning being initiated from a centralised system run by the Air Ministry using a combination of Observer Corps Posts located throughout the country and later by radar stations sited around the coasts. Air raid shelters in the form of trenches were dug in open spaces and were the first manifestation of a policy to protect people everywhere from the effects of bomb blast and flying debris. The trenches were followed soon after by the construction of basement shelters created by shoring up existing cellars, and then various designs of surface shelter, usually of brick and concrete construction. A gas attack was prepared for by the issue of gas masks to every individual and the construction of new, or adaptation of existing, facilities to provide gas decontamination buildings where showers would be available and contaminated clothing could be laundered. Air raid wardens were appointed to ensure that a general lighting blackout was observed and to direct people caught out-of-doors during a raid to the nearest shelters. Fire services were augmented by the addition of an Auxiliary Fire Service formed from trained volunteers, later to be combined with the formerly local authority run fire services to form the National Fire Service. Fire fighting equipment in the form of trailer pumps and large towing cars were provided for use by the AFS throughout both urban and rural areas. First Aid facilities in the form of unmanned 'points', where medical materials were stored in readiness for an attack, and 'posts', which were to be manned at all times by a doctor and nurses, were provided at key points.[20]

A large government-run munitions factory like Blackpole, which would employ several thousand people, would have had most of these facilities provided on both the factory site and in the workers' housing, although no detailed documentary evidence for these facilities has been found. No communal air raid precaution facilities such as shelters have survived, but the structure of the staff housing at Tolladine was designed to provide some protection from bombing.

However, it is known that roof spotters were used at Blackpole, whose role was to spot the arrival of enemy aircraft and warn the workforce of imminent attack. It had been found elsewhere in Britain that using the more general public air raid warning system of sirens to indicate the beginning and end of an air alert wasted a great deal of factory production time. The idea behind the roof spotters was that they would leave the warning until the last possible moment when enemy aircraft were actually seen approaching the factory, and the workforce would only then leave their work stations to go the nearest air raid shelters. The spotters were all volunteers and were trained in aircraft recognition so that only the sight of enemy aircraft should precipitate a warning. Most large factories formed spotter clubs, that for the Blackpole factory being numbered 719. The spotters acquired the name Jim Crows.[21]

From May 1940, when a German invasion of Britain by paratroops and airborne troops followed by ground forces landed from the sea seemed imminent, a local defence force was formed from volunteers aged between 17 and 65, to be called the Local Defence Volunteers. This force was quickly renamed the Home Guard and organised along the lines of the Regular Army. Worcester City raised a battalion of over 2,000 men, one of 12 battalions in Worcestershire, each with a hierarchy of companies, platoons and sections. Most factories raised a platoon or section, some in the county even having enough volunteers to form a company. The Blackpole factory was no exception and formed No.6 Platoon under the command of Lieutenant L. Court, part of B Company of the 1st Worcestershire (Worcester City) Battalion.

The role of No.6 Platoon was firstly to protect the factory against both air and ground attack by enemy forces. It was easy to envisage that the Germans might, for example, attempt to capture the nearby Perdiswell airfield by use of parachutists followed up by

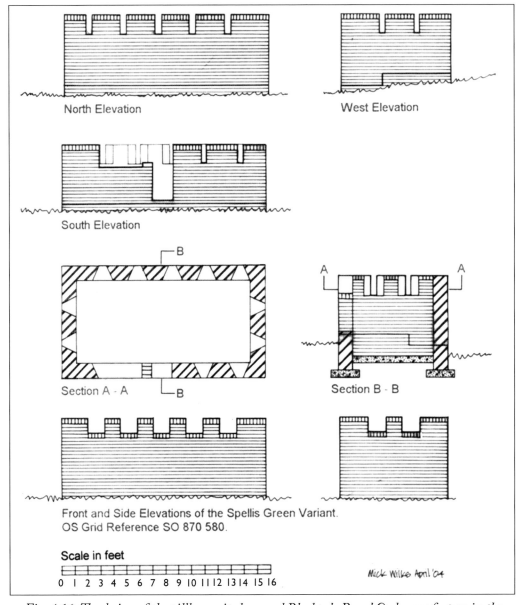

Fig. 4.16 The design of the pillboxes sited around Blackpole Royal Ordnance factory in the Second World War

Fig. 4.17 Now a rare survivor, this pillbox stands on one of the fairways of the golf course to the west of the Blackpole trading estate. It has the same open-topped design as many others built in the Worcester area during 1940, most of which have long since been demolished. This pillbox would have provided a defence post for Home Guards defending the western approaches used by any invading enemy troops attacking the Blackpole munitions factory. In addition to defending against any ground troops, the open-topped design would allow them to fire in the air at enemy parachutists. (Photo by Mick Wilks, 2004)

air-landed troops using the ubiquitous three-engine Junkers Ju 52 transport aircraft, before a more general attack on Worcester City was made by armoured columns in much the same way as Holland, Belgium and France had been attacked. The paratroops and air-landed troops would have fanned out, capturing factories as they went. To help the Home Guards at Blackpole protect their factory, it would have been usual to have mounted a number of automatic weapons on the factory roofs in order to fire at low flying aircraft. Commonly these would have been Lewis guns arranged in pairs on stalk mountings. A circle of at least six small brick fortifications were constructed in the fields around the factory to provide protected firing points for Home Guard riflemen from which to deter enemy troops attempting to infiltrate the factory from the nearby fields. Three of these small pillboxes still exist, each of an unusual design without the normal concrete roof (see Figs. 4.16 and 4.17). This open-topped design seems to be peculiar to Worcester and implies that they would have allowed the occupying riflemen to have fired into the air at the descending parachutists. In addition to these pillboxes, there are likely to have been trench systems and weapons pits, but only scanty documentary evidence exists to tell us where some were sited around the Blackpole factory.[22] However, Figure 4.18 showing the adjoining Perdiswell airfield defences, for which documentary evidence does exist, provides a measure of the extent of such defences around a defended locality.

Because of its importance as a munitions factory, Blackpole was designated as a Vulnerable Point which highlighted the need for protection from enemy interference or sabotage. Therefore, besides the more conventional military defences, the Home Guard would also have had a role in protecting the factory against saboteurs and enemy agents. This would involve the Home Guards manning road blocks on the approaches to the factory in order to check the bona fides of people wishing to enter the site, a role shared with other Home Guard units in the vicinity as well as the War Department

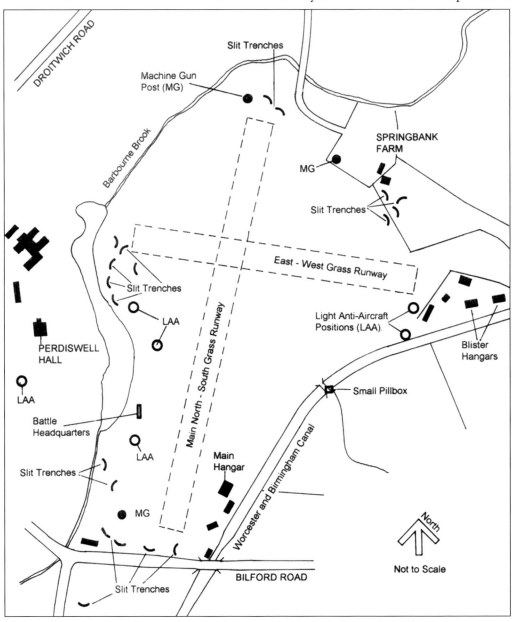

Fig. 4.18 The range of defences provided in the Second World War at Royal Air Force Worcester, Perdiswell

Constabulary who would be present at the main gates to the complex.[23] In addition, the factory Home Guard would be responsible for patrolling the perimeter fence each night to ensure that agents or saboteurs were not trying to 'get under the wire'. They would also have had a role, along with their comrades from the Ward and Archdale factories, in manning the nearby road blocks as part of the outer defences of Worcester City Anti-tank Island.[24]

Clifford Lord recalls joining the Blackpole factory Home Guard platoon in 1942 whereupon he was invited by Captain Phillips to join the factory bomb disposal squad and become a member of the 'Suicide Club' (see below)! Of his time in the Home Guard, Clifford remembers that there was no choice in the matter, everyone had to join. He describes a very obvious class distinction in the force, with the bosses being the officers, ex-First World War veterans being the NCOs and the other ranks being made up of the blue collar workers.

The Blackpole platoon was apparently well trained in infantry weapons, including the Ross rifle and the Sten machine-carbine, at either the Tyddesley Wood Range or at the Barclays Brickworks at Merriman's Hill. If a grouping of four inches could be achieved at 200 yards on the range with a Ross rifle, then the individual would be rewarded with the issue of a Lee Enfield which, in Clifford's view, was a much better weapon. He also used the EY Projector (a device fitted to an infantry rifle for projecting the standard Mills Bomb) and threw live grenades at Tyddesley Wood. Bayonet drill was also practised using straw stuffed sandbags on a wooden structure. He recalls having indoor instruction about grenades by a Sergeant Phillips. Each man was given a grenade and shown how to fit a detonator and arm a grenade. During one lecture, Sergeant Phillips, who had at some time lost some of the fingers from the hand he was using to grip the grenade, pulled the pin from the grenade and Clifford recalls the scramble of men sitting near the front to get near the back of the room!

Clifford recalled that any Home Guard who did not perform his duties satisfactorily would be called before an officer and would have his hat snatched off as a means of humiliation.

The Bomb Disposal Section

Blackpole factory was one of half a dozen factories and establishments in Worcestershire that organised a bomb disposal section under the direction of a Royal Engineer officer. In the case of the Blackpole Factory, this was a Captain A.W. Phillips. Formed initially throughout Britain in December 1940 at the height of the blitz, these civilian volunteers were intended to provide support for Royal Engineer (RE) bomb disposal teams. They would come under the orders of, and would be trained by, the Royal Engineers. Formed of 15 or so men, these squads were transferred to the Home Guard in June 1941.

The role of the factory bomb disposal squads was to establish safety zones around unexploded bombs, enforce crowd control and carry out preliminary excavations so that RE Bomb Disposal Units could more readily deal with the bombs, thereby speeding the return to production. After the intense and thorough technical training that Clifford Lord received as part of the Bomb Disposal Squad, he was not too keen on the more conventional arms drill. He particularly suffered with the pain felt in his collar bone from the weight of the rifle banging down on his shoulder. He tried putting cloth pads inside his shirt, but all this achieved was the rifle hitting his neck.[25]

To reduce night bombing raids on vulnerable targets such as Blackpole, at least 18 bombing decoy sites were located in Worcestershire, most of them created to protect munitions industries in Birmingham and the Black Country, the county being on the flight path of the Luftwaffe on their way to those targets. Two of the decoy sites were specifically created to divert bombers away from Worcester, one located in open countryside adjacent to the River Teme, north of Brockamin, the other on Kempsey Common. By a combination of various forms of decoy fires, and in the case of that at Brockamin the addition of mock factory lighting, it was hoped that German bombers would be encouraged to drop their bombs on open fields instead of the local factories.[26]

Although the site at Blackpole was not itself bombed during the Second World War, a raid by a single German aircraft in 1940 dropped a total of three bombs nearby. One of the bombs damaged a house in Highland Road, Tunnel Hill, while another landed in King George's playing field. As a small boy, the late author recalled inspecting the crater in the playing field.[27]

Feeding and entertaining the Blackpole workers

Mrs Kathleen Halford (née Telfer) was first employed in service in Birmingham but moved with her employer to Upton upon Severn. At the age of 17 she was directed to work at the Blackpole factory. She continued to live in Upton and used the works bus

Fig. 4.19 A wedding party of Second World War munitions workers from Blackpole, somewhere in Worcester. On the right in the second row is Annie Bilby; none of the others have been identified. (Courtesy of Doreen Stevenson)

service to travel to the factory. There she was employed in the canteen, helping to serve meals and washing plates and dishes, as well as making sandwiches. Another of her tasks was to provide a trolley service taking drinks and snacks around the factory. She recalls that the factory was so noisy that it was necessary to shout all the time. One of her colleagues was May Bailey, who had a good Irish voice and would sing Sophie Tucker songs to cheer up the staff in the canteen. Kathleen was married in 1942 and left later that year to have a child.

Peggy Law (née Rann) remembers that the canteen was a large single-storey building and incorporated a stage at one end. Here visiting celebrities, such as Vera Lynn, Wendy Miller and others, would entertain the workers on the morning shift in their lunch break. Part of the entertainment at the factory was constant music played through loud speakers, including the BBC's 'Workers Playtime', to help the girls get through the long hours of tedious work on the production lines. The girls could make requests for particular songs and Clifford Lord remembers that he and his friends in the MED team became fed up with hearing Vera Lynn singing 'There'll be Bluebirds Over the White Cliffs of Dover', which was regularly requested. To stop the sound, Jock Kelly pulled some of the wires from the loudspeakers which were fixed in the roof structure. These had to be quickly replaced because it turned out that the wires also carried power to other parts of the factory!

Visits to the factory by celebrities was one means used of keeping up the morale of the workforce and Jimmie Wild, a professional boxer, is one of those remembered as coming.

Clifford recalls that the men and women were well fed in the works canteen, steamed puddings being one of their specialities, and not a ration book in sight! The canteens' location on the site (there was one for men and one for women) are as yet unidentified by any of the witnesses to those times, but Clifford thought that they were in a long narrow building on the east side of the railway.

Peggy Law recalls that the girls were given weekend breaks about every six weeks, and that during the summer months farmers would send out lorries to take volunteer workers for pea picking or other similar jobs out on the farms, when it was grand to get out in the fresh air after working long hours in the factory. Otherwise, for entertainment, there were two good cinemas in Worcester – The Scala in Angel Place and The Gaumont in Foregate Street. For worship, she and her friends would go in a group to St Nicholas's Church in The Foregate. These friends came from all over Britain. Apart from Margaret, her long-standing friend from Burgess Hill who came to Worcester with her, they included Florrie, who came from Scotland and two sisters, Lil and Mair, from Wales. Sometimes they would be joined by two local girls, one from Worcester, the other from Malvern. One of their highlights was going to dances at an unidentified American Army base which would send coaches to pick up the girls from the hostel. Apart from enjoying the dancing, the refreshments, with varieties of cakes, were apparently delicious. Train trips to the Malvern Hills were another opportunity to get out into fresh air, and sometimes she would return to her family in Sussex during the weekend breaks.

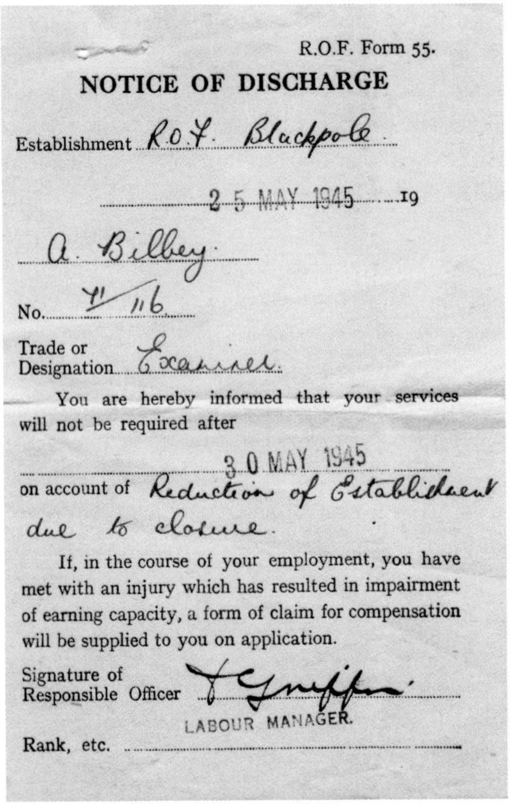

R.O.F. Form 55.

NOTICE OF DISCHARGE

Establishment *R.O.F. Blackpole.*

2 5 MAY 1945 19

A. Bilbey.

No. *Y 116*

Trade or
Designation *Examiner.*

You are hereby informed that your services
will not be required after

3 0 MAY 1945

on account of *Reduction of Establishment
due to closure.*

If, in the course of your employment, you have
met with an injury which has resulted in impairment
of earning capacity, a form of claim for compensation
will be supplied to you on application.

Signature of
Responsible Officer

LABOUR MANAGER.

Rank, etc.

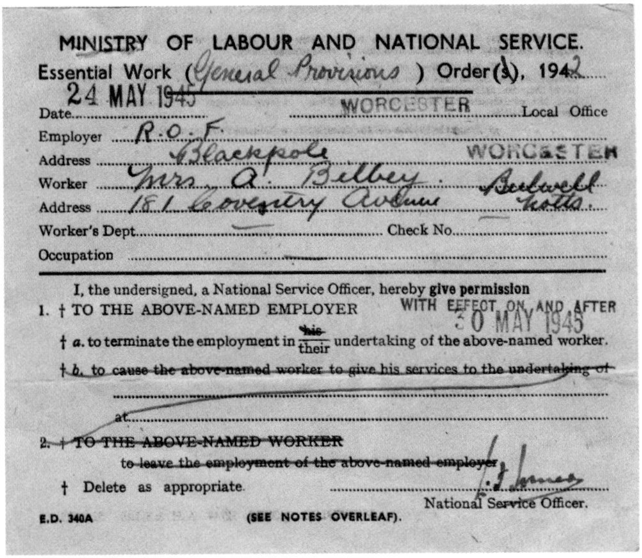

MINISTRY OF LABOUR AND NATIONAL SERVICE.

Essential Work (*General Provisions*) Order(s), 1942.

24 MAY 1945
Date................................ WORCESTER ....Local Office
Employer ....*R.O.F.*
Address ....*Blackpole*............ WORCESTER
Worker ....*Mrs A. Bilbey*....*Bedwell*
Address ....*181 Coventry Avenue*....*Notts*
Worker's Dept................................ Check No.................
Occupation ....

I, the undersigned, a National Service Officer, hereby **give permission**
1. † TO THE ABOVE-NAMED EMPLOYER WITH EFFECT ON AND AFTER
   3 0 MAY 1945
   † a. to terminate the employment in ~~the~~ their undertaking of the above-named worker.
   † b. to cause the above-named worker to give his services to the undertaking of

....
   at ....

2. † TO THE ABOVE-NAMED WORKER
      to leave the employment of the above-named employer
   † Delete as appropriate. ....
                                        National Service Officer.
E.D. 340A   (SEE NOTES OVERLEAF).

Victory in Europe (VE) Day at Blackpole

Peggy Law remembers that she heard of the end of the war in Europe when one of the girls in the hostel came running down the corridor shouting out the news. The victory was later celebrated with a bonfire on the green traffic island on the corner of Field Road and Blackpole Road, just to the south of the Wards factory, and opposite the main entrance to the hostel. Although there was no alcohol available on the green at the time, they were nevertheless in high spirits and swinging each other round, cheering and dancing around the fire and on the adjoining roads. She recalls that it was a wonderful feeling and fuelled by pure high spirits. Later the crowd headed for the local pub, presumably The New Chequers on the corner of Astwood Road and Brickfields Road. On leaving Worcester in 1945, Peggy pursued a career in market gardening to which she had been transferred. Now living in Rochdale, Lancashire, Peggy is still in touch with her friend Margaret in Burgess Hill, and her Scottish friend from the Blackpole days.

Fig. 4.20 Mrs Annie Bilby's discharge papers from Blackpole ROF, issued just 21 days after VE Day. (Courtesy of Doreen Stevenson)

5   POST-WAR BLACKPOLE

It was towards the end of 1945 that Cadbury's started to take repossession of the buildings at Blackpole, although the Admiralty and the Ministry of Supply retained three of the buildings for storage use, including Building 11 again. The Bournville works magazine described the moves as gradual but by November 1946 Cadbury's had brought back some of the equipment and machinery that had been kept at Bournville during the war, supplemented by new, more efficient, machinery. Initially, work at the Blackpole factory was on a small scale, with the manufacture, by women operators, of tins for Cocoa, Bournvita and other products for despatch to Bournville. By November 1946 they were producing three million tins a week. The process of sorting, cleaning and roasting of almond and hazel nuts for use in the manufacture of chocolate bars was also developing

Fig. 5.1 The nut store was one of the first of the Cadbury uses to return to Blackpole after the Second World War. This image is dated November 1945. (Courtesy of Worcester News*)*

Fig. 5.2 Women of Cadbury's Cake Division at work at the Blackpole factory, making what appear to be 'Biscuit Delight' cakes, apparently a very tasty layered sponge cake, filled with cream and jam. (Courtesy of Worcester News)

at Blackpole. A new nut-roasting machine could apparently handle tons of nuts each day. Marzipan-making machinery was also in the process of being reinstalled.

Mr L.S. Young, a long-time Bournville employee was in charge, with Miss D. Griffin as the 'Forewoman' and Mr H. W. Mitchell as the 'Foreman'. Many of their previous staff had returned and, together with newcomers, about 150 men and women were employed at Blackpole by 1947. The factory was seen as having the potential to become an important employer of women in the Worcester area. The management was taking every step to improve amenities at the factory, with a canteen supplying mid-day meals, a recreation hall used for dancing, and the formation of an active sports club. Through the Ministry of Labour, girls had also arrived from south Wales and the north of England to work there.[1]

In 1962 the Blackpole factory was chosen as the site for Cadbury's cake making operation. Four years later, however, the Board of Trade refused to issue an industrial development certificate for the expansion of the complex with a completely new cake making factory on the grounds that there was a need to tackle serious unemployment elsewhere. As a result cake production was shared with the company's Morton site on the Wirral near Liverpool. This was described by local newspapers as 'sounding the first death-knell for the company's operation at Worcester'. By 1967 Cadbury's were part of a group of companies called the British Cocoa and Chocolate Company Ltd, comprising the Cadbury, Fry and Pascall Group. In August 1971 the workforce was handed a dupli-cated letter explaining that the need for economies in the group, by then known as Cadbury-Schweppes Ltd, would result in the closure of the factory after a merger with United Biscuits Ltd (trading as McVitie) and the move of all cake production to the

Morton site. Cake production at Blackpole ceased in May 1972 with the loss of almost 680 jobs, 320 of which had been occupied part-time by married women. The factory was closed by the company soon afterwards, the event being described by one union official as the biggest industrial tragedy Worcester had ever seen. Most of the Blackpole site was sold off in 1974 to the Grosvenor Square Property Company for £1,000,000.[2]

During the early post-war period the late author's wife, Sylvia, recalls that chocolate crumb was transported by barge from Gloucester Docks up to Blackpole by river and canal. While still a young girl, she and her friends would visit relatives who lived close-by and witnessed the bargees, complete with their families who lived on the boats, unloading the crumb. On one occasion, and seeing the cut garden flowers that Sylvia was taking to her relatives, the bargees offered to exchange chocolate crumb for some of the blooms in order to decorate the boats. Sylvia remembers that the crumb was very nice to eat and a welcome addition to their diet in the then ration-book Britain.

Sylvia went on to work at Blackpole from 1957 to 1962. During this time she recalls that the factory handled a number of processes for Cadbury's. Besides the cakes, which included the popular Biscuit Delight, a thin sponge sandwich with cream and jam filling, illustrated in the adjacent photograph (Fig. 5.2), Cadbury's Chocolate Selection and Easter Eggs were also packaged there. Sylvia recalls bars of Fry's chocolate-covered Turkish Delight being made at Blackpole, as well as shop-window displays of faux Cadbury's products. The former Bullet Shop was the focus for most of the Cadbury processes, with the offices at the front being reused for that purpose, and the area behind them divided up into four separate rooms. Cake production was located in the southern part of the building, with the Raisin Room alongside, while behind them was the Tin Production Room and the Nut Room. The back (western end) of the main building adjoining the covered railway sidings was used for storage of in-coming materials and outgoing products.

To get to work at Blackpole, Sylvia would use Midland Red Omnibus Company special services, which would pick up workers from around the residential areas of Worcester, timed to arrive at the factory for the start and finish of the working day. Some of the men at the factory would apparently work through the night, loading and unloading goods, presumably received or despatched by rail and taking advantage of the rail siding down from the main line which still existed then, and when main-line passenger services were not running.

In Sylvia's time at Cadbury's, the works canteen was located in a long, narrow building on the west side of the railway embankment, reached on foot from the main factory buildings via the underpass (this is likely to be a reuse of the original munitions factory canteen facility and was possibly the building immediately to the west of Building 11, although it has yet to be positively identified as such). While the narrow gauge railway system within the site was still intact in the 1950s and '60s, it was no longer used.[3]

At some point Norcros Properties Ltd acquired the Blackpole site and the Hygena kitchen furniture manufacturers moved into the former cake-making factory in January 1973 in a mood of apparent optimism. Some 300 people were taken on and another 500 were expected to join them. Subsequently, the Liverpool-based company found that there was a nationwide glut of kitchen furniture and new orders were not being

Fig. 5.3 Hygena, the kitchen furniture manufacturer occupied the Blackpole factory after Cadbury-Schweppes sold the site. Flat-packed units are being assembled prior to despatch.
(Courtesy of Worcester News)

received. After being run down over a short period, during which it incurred some labour problems and picketing of the site by disaffected workers, Hygena closed their Blackpole factory on 1 April 1977.[4]

Cadbury Schweppes still retained a small interest in the Blackpole site after the main sale to the Grosvenor Square Property Company in the form of a transport services depot, employing about 15 people, which had been operating since 1973. Its closure came in 1982 as part of a streamlining plan to reduce the company's depots from five to three nationwide.[5]

The largest of the original First World War Cartridge Factory No.3 buildings still exists at Blackpole, as well as Building 11, and are now incorporated in, and surrounded by, much new commercial development to form part of the trading estates of Blackpole East and Blackpole West run by Lansdowne Rodway Estates. Remnants of the narrow gauge railway of the

Fig. 5.4 Remnants of the 2ft gauge light railway track that served the various elements of the Blackpole site can still be seen, such as this short section here.
(Photo by Mick Wilks, 2015)

First World War period can still be found on the site, together with the brick arch carrying the mainline railway over the route of the narrow gauge railway between the east and west parts of the original munitions factory. Of the Blackpole Halt platforms and signal box on the main line, nothing remains, or indeed of the Astwood Halt a little way to the south, although remnants of the wharfing can still be seen alongside the canal. The bungalows constructed by the Cadbury Company on the extreme west of the Blackpole site are still there, but are now surrounded by high hedges.

Fig. 5.5 The east front of the Blackpole munitions factory is little changed from when it was built in 1916. This is the main building of the original works and forms the core of Landsdowne Rodway Estates' East Blackpole trading estate. (Photo by Colin Jones)

Fig. 5.6 The gable ends on this elevation of the west half of the main munitions factory indicate that this building still has its clerestorey roof lighting structures in place. (Photo by Mick Wilks, 2015)

A Memorial – at last!

Women were generally the unsung heroes of both world wars and many, as we have seen, did not receive a medal for the effort they made towards the victories in either conflict. In the past, while many other countries had monuments to the women who had contributed to their war effort, Britain did not. A fund-raising scheme to provide such a monument to Britain's women who served in various capacities in the Second World War was led by the fund's patron, Baroness Boothroyd, with Dame Vera Lynn, the Princess Royal and a number of other prominent people acting as vice patrons. Together with substantial contributions from the National Heritage Lottery Fund and the Memorial to the Women of World War II Fund based in York, over £1,000,000 was raised. The completed monument to The Women of World War II was unveiled in Whitehall on 9 July 2005 by Queen Elizabeth II and dedicated by Baroness Boothroyd, as part of the commemoration of the 60th anniversary of the end of the war.

Fig. 5.7 The memorial to the women of the Second World War in Whitehall. (Photo by Paul Turner)

The bronze monument includes 17 representations of the uniforms of women of the main armed forces as well as the Women's Land Army, nursing, police and civil defence services, but most importantly also the women industrial workers represented by a welding mask. The sculpting of the bronze monument was carried out by John W. Mills and the unveiling ceremony was attended by many women veterans of the Second World War. The flypast that day included a number of helicopters and two Tornado jet fighters, all flown by women.

The monument stands 22 feet high, 16 feet long and 6 feet wide, while the lettering on the sides is in the same style as wartime ration books.

6   CONCLUSIONS

In their usual enthusiastic, but in many ways arrogant fashion, the British went to war with Germany in 1914 full of optimism that it would all be over by Christmas. It was very quickly realised that the Germans were a much tougher nut to crack than had been first thought and that the war was going to be much longer than expected. Throughout history British governments appear to have been ill prepared for each successive war, and tend to fight the current war with the last war's technology! The recent experiences in the Middle East, with troops having to buy some of their kit, suggest that some things don't really change. The story of 1914 was no different, when inadequate numbers of troops were sent to war with inadequate equipment against the vastly bigger and better equipped German Army, and when the undoubted professionalism and courage of the British soldier was no substitute for proper preparation. As a consequence, the lives of most of the experienced pre-war regulars of the army were lost in the early battles on the Western Front. To give it its due, the government of the day set about enlarging the army and manufacturing the necessary equipment with speed and good management until in 1918, a war-winning, all-arms, army had been created and the whole of the adult population of Britain had become involved in what became recognised as total war. Situated in the countryside on the north side of Worcester, on either side of the former Great Western (Bristol to Birmingham) Railway Line, the Blackpole munitions factory was born out of that early war crisis.

The main buildings of the original First World War munitions factory still survive at Blackpole, and the special housing for some of the Blackpole workers, built during the Second World War, can also still be seen to the south of Tolladine Road. All of these buildings are important reminders of how Britain, when sufficiently motivated, can achieve great things and as such they should be cherished!

APPENDIX

EMPLOYMENT FIGURES FOR BLACKPOLE
IN THE SECOND WORLD WAR[1]

28th September 1940	50
28th December 1940	594
11th January 1941	629
29th March 1941	927
21st March 1942	2,182
May 1942	2,709 of whom 1954 were women
17th December 1942	3,936 on the payroll of whom the factory staff were 3,867
January 1943	3,242
March 1943	An unspecified number of employees were mobile workers transferred from Hereford to Blackpole.
April 1943	3,602
May 1943	3,524
June 1943	3,484
July 1943	3,436
August 1943	3,418
September 1943	3,301
October 1943	3,205 of whom 2,505 were women
November 1943	2,217 of whom 1,555 were women
December 1943	2,072
January 1943	1,985
February 1944	1,945
March 1944	1,906
April 1944	1,873 of whom 1,327 were women
May 1944	1,590
June 1944	1,471
July 1944	1,545 of whom 984 were women
August 1944	1,503 of whom 984 were women
September 1944	1,113 of whom 703 were women
October 1944	717
November 1944	683 of whom 364 were women
December 1944	666
January 1945	651 of whom 340 were women
March 1945	623 of whom 340 were women
April 1945	618 of whom 323 were women
May 1945	596 of whom 312 were women
June 1945	207 of whom 25 were women.

BIBLIOGRAPHY AND SOURCES OF INFORMATION

Books and Manuscripts

Anonymous. *The Official History of the Ministry of Munitions. Vol VIII - Control of Industrial Capacity and Equipment and Vol XI The Supply of Munitions.* (Naval and Military Press Ltd, East Sussex, undated).

Barnett, Correlli. *Britain and Her Army 1509-1970. A Military, Political and Social Survey.* (Publisher's details not available).

Beckett, Dr Ian and Chandler, Dr David (eds). *The Oxford Illustrated History of the British Army.* (Oxford University Press undated).

Cocroft, Wayne. *Dangerous Energy.* (English Heritage, Swindon, 2000)

Dewar, George A.B. *The Great War Munitions Feat 1914-1918.* (Constable and Co. Ltd, London, 1921)

Dickson, Sally (Kidderminster & District Archaeological and Historical Society). *Great War Britain - Kidderminster Remembering 1914-18.* (The History Press, Stroud, 2014)

Griffiths,Gareth. *Women's Factory Work in World War I.* (Alan Sutton Publishing Co., Stroud, 1991)

Harris, Carol. *Women Under Fire in World War Two.* (BBC.co.uk/history)

Hornby, William. *History of the Second World War - Factories and Plant.* (HMSO, London, 1958)

Love, Lt-Colonel C.P. (retired). 'Trouble in the Wind - The History of the Worcestershire Territorial Battalions 1919-1967'. (Unpublished document held in the Mercian Regiment Museum)

Mitchell, J. and Keith Smith. *From Worcester to Birmingham.* (Middleton Press, Sussex, 2007).

Taylor, A.J.P. *English History 1914-1918.* (Oxford University Press, 1965).

Thompson, Melvyn. *Woven in Kidderminster.* (David Vine Associates, Kidderminster, 2002)

Warner, Philip. *World War One; A Chronological Narrative.* (Arms and Armour Press, London, 1998).

Wilks, M. *The Defence of Worcestershire and the Southern Approaches to Birmingham.* (Logaston Press, Herefordshire, 2007).

Wilks, M. *Chronicles of the Worcestershire Home Guard.* (Logaston Press, Herefordshire, 2014)

National Archive Files consulted by Colin Jones with limited success

AVIA - 12/11, 22/768, 22/1034, 22/1046, 22/1084, 22/1100, 22/1161, 22/1249, 22/1267, 22/1268, 22/1270, 22/1275,22/1292, 22/1309, 22/3012, 38/394, 46/194, 46/276, 46/278, 46/279, 46/284, 46/297, 46/309, 46/320, 50/88, 53/1.

CAB - 27/604, 102/273, 102/355, 102/357, 102/359, 102/624, 102/625, 102/627, 102/630, 102/631, 102/632, 102/633, 115/637.

EF - 5/20.

HLG - 90/12.

HO - 192/56, 205/336.

LAB - 9/96, 22/55, 22/63, 22/64, 26/13, 26/17, 26/38, 26/39, 26/188.

MT - 6/2496/2, 6/2499/9.

MUN - 4/1703, 4/2217, 4/2243, 4/2244, 4/6361, 4/6296, 5/10, 5/57, 5/105, 5/365, 5/366, 7/408.

RAIL - 282/1435, 864/9, 864/10, 864/10, 864/16.

SUPP - 5/990, 5/1260.

T - 162/726.

WO - 166/6822, 193/477.

WORK - 22/148.

Worcestershire Archive and Archaeology Service files consulted
BA 10465, b496.5, Part 72

BA 11898. 705:1265

REFERENCES

1 Introduction
1. From *World War One A Chronological Narrative* by Philip Warner.
2. Following the Boer War, the Worcestershire Regiment was one of a number of regiments which had been expanded to four regular battalions as a result of its good recruiting record.
3. From *Mud, Blood and Poppycock* by Gordon Corrigan, pages 40 and 48.
4. ibid.
5. The War Memoirs of David Lloyd-George.
6. From the *Great War Munitions Feat* by George Dewar.
7. Primarily from the War Memoirs of David Lloyd George.
8. ibid.

2 Blackpole and the First World War
1. From *The History of the Second World War - Factories and Plant* by William Hornby.
2. From Kings Norton Metal Company Minutes held by Birmingham Record Office, file number RO MS 1422/32/1/7/4.
3. ibid.
4. Most of this section was gleaned from the *Official Histories of the Ministry of Munitions*. Vols VIII and XI.
5. *Worcester Daily Times*, 27 January 1917 and pers. comm. of Clifford Lord interviewed on 23 November 2015.
6. *Worcester Daily Times*, 5 July 1916.
7. From Streets Committee Minutes held by the County Archive Section under BA 11241, Box No 4 E22.
8. Pers. comm. Clifford Lord, interviewed on 23 November 2015.
9. From Kings Norton Metal Company Minutes.
10. Primarily from the *Official Histories of the Ministry of Munitions*.
11. From 'The .303 British Service Cartridge' by Roy Tebbutt, *Harrington Aviation Magazine* Vol.3 No.1.
12. From Ministry of Munitions statistics.
13. From *Dangerous Energy* by Wayne Cockroft.
14. From TNA File MUN 4/6361).
15. *Worcester Daily Times*, Saturday 13 January 1917.
16. *Worcester Daily Times*, Saturday 23 and Monday 25 February 1918.
17. TNA File MT6/2496/2 and *From Worcester to Birmingham* by Vic Mitchell and Keith Smith.
18. From TNA File RAIL 864/16.
19. *Worcester Daily Times*, 19 April 1917.
20. *Worcester Daily Times*, Friday 27 October 1916.
21. From County Archive Ref BA11898. 705.1265.
22. *Worcester Daily Times*, Monday 6 January 1917.

23. *Worcester Daily Times*, 2 July 1917.
24. *Worcester Daily Times*, 3 November 1916.
25. *Worcester Daily Times*, 4 October 1917.
26. *Worcester Daily Times*, 7 May 1917.
27. *Worcester Daily Times*, Friday 13 December and *Berrow's Worcester Journal*, Saturday 21 December 1918.
28. *Worcester Daily Times*, Thursday 25 July, Saturday 27 July and Monday 29 July 1918.
29. From *Kidderminster Remembered 1914-18* by Sally Dickson and Kidderminster and District Archaeological and Historical Society, page 124.
30. *Worcester Daily Times*, Tuesday 12 November 1918.
31. *Worcester Daily Times*, Wednesday 13 November 1918.
32. *Worcester Daily Times*, Thursday 14 November 1918.
33. *Women's Factory Work* by Gareth Griffiths, pages 6, 56 and 57.
34. *Worcester Herald*, 14 December 1918.

3 Blackpole between the Wars

1. TNA Files CAB 102/624 and AVIA 46/279.
2. From Hansard, 28 July 1919.
3. Kings Norton Metal Company Minutes.
4. From the Supplement to the *London Gazette*, 30 March 1920.
5. *Berrow's Worcester Journal*, Saturday 13 September 1919.
6. *Worcester Daily Times*, Saturday 20 December 1919.
7. From Kings Norton Metal Company Minutes.
8. *Worcester Herald* and *Berrow's Worcester Journal*, Saturday 16 April 1921 and the *Worcester Herald*, 23 April.
9. *Worcester Herald*, Saturday 23 April 1921.
10. *Berrow's Worcester Journal*, Saturday 8 June 1921.
11. *Journal of Contemporary History*. Vol.6 No.2; 'The British Government's Strike Breaking Organisation and Black Friday' by Ralph Desmarais, from *Trouble in the Wind* by Lt-Col C.P. Love and *Berrow's Worcester Journal*, Saturday 23 April 1921.
12. TNA Files AVIA 53/1 and AVIA 46/284, and CRO File BA11 898 .705 Pt 1265.
13. From the Cadbury Archive.
14. *Worcester Evening News and Times*, 29 November 1946.
15. *Berrow's Worcester News*, May 1926.
16. *Worcester Evening News and Times*, 29 November 1945.
17. CRO BA 11898. 705. 1265.

4 Blackpole in the Second World War

1. TNA File AVIA 46/279.
2. TNA File AVIA 46/320.
3. TNA File AVIA 46/284 and the Cadbury Archive.
4. TNA File AVIA 46/320 and from *Woven in Kidderminster* by Melvyn Thompson.
5. TNA files CAB 102/623 and AVIA 46/194.

6. TNA Files AVIA 46/194, CAB 102/273, CAB102/633 and HO 192/56.
7. TNA File Supp. 5/1260.
8. *Worcester Evening News and Times*, 4 January 1943; TNA File SUPP 5/1260, information from the Ministry of Defence Medal Office, and the *London Gazette* Supplement, 4 January 1943.
9. TNA Files AVIA 22/1084, 22/1161, 22/1292 and 53/1.
10. TNA File AVIA53/1.
11. From an interview with Bryan and Ann Massie on 21 September 2016.
12. From correspondence with her daughter, Val Davies and Peggy Law from 2015 onwards.
13. From interviews of Clifford Lord on 16 April 2012 and again on 23 November 2015.
14. TNA Files AVIA 46/309, 50/48, LAB22/63.
15. TNA File LAB 26/188.
16. Worcester City Council planning records.
17. CRO File Ref: BA 10465, b 496.5, Pt 72.
18. From an article by Finn Jenson in *Cambridge Journals*, 2008.
19. Telephone conversation with Ken Murton, 6 July 2009.
20. From *20th Century Defences in the West Midlands* by Colin Jones, Bernard Lowry & Mick Wilks.
21. Pers. comm. by the late Maurice Jones.
22. See *The Defence of Worcestershire and the Southern Approaches to Birmingham* by Mick Wilks
23. TNA File WO 166//6822.
24. See *The Defence of Worcestershire and the Southern Approaches to Birmingham* by Mick Wilks.
25. From *The Chronicles of the Worcestershire Home Guard* by Mick Wilks.
26. From *The Defence of Worcestershire and the Southern Approaches to Birmingham* by Mick Wilks.
27. *Worcester Evening News and Times*, 30 September 2011 and pers. comm. of Colin Jones.

5 Post-War Blackpole

1. *Worcester Evening News and Times*, 29 November 1945 and 29 November 1946, and the Bournville works magazine of February 1947.
2. *Worcester Evening News*, 10 and 17 February 1967, 21 December 1972, 12 January 1973 and 22 January 2010.
3. Pers. comm. from Sylvia Jones interviewed on 7 February 2016.
4. *Worcester Evening News*, 4 and 6 December 1976, and 1 April 1977.
5. *Worcester Evening News*, 8 May 1981.

Appendix

1. TNA Files AVIA 22/1161, 22/1292 and 22/1084.

INDEX

83

The Story of Worcester
by Pat Hughes & Annette Leech
Paperback, 320 pages, 140 colour and 90 b/w illustrations   £15

Here are gathered many tales of the city and its inhabitants over the centuries: events and person-alities from visiting monarchs to food riots, from a friar who was found up to no good in the Cardinal's Hat, to crowds flocking to see an amazing learned dog who could 'read, write and keep accounts'. Trades and tradesmen, crime and punishment, building and rebuilding, the pattern of the streets and the ever present great River Severn. Whether caught up on the fringes of the Wars of the Roses or besieged in the Civil War, Worcester keeps going – and growing, as its traditional trades are joined by the arrival of newer industries. The story tells of both the rich and the poor, city officials and felons condemned to transportation, the idle and the industrious, tales gleaned from their extensive research among the city's archives, and illustrated with a wealth of photographs, paintings, drawings and plans.

The Story of Norton Barracks
Home of the Worcestershire Regiment
by Stan Jobson
Paperback, 112 pages with 65 black and white photos   £7.50

This is the story of both the buildings that formed Norton Barracks and of the soldiers and other personnel who were based there as members of staff or who passed through as they underwent training. Stan Jobson has spent much time in the Regimental Archives unearthing both photo-graphs and personal recollections of time spent at the barracks. The result is a tale of British Military history in microcosm, but often seen from a personal viewpoint of hard training, military structures, playful pranks, sporting achievements, patriotic surges, post D-Day traumas and both keen and reluctant National Servicemen.

Chronicles of the Worcestershire Home Guard
by Mick Wilks
Paperback, 368 pages, over 140 b/w photographs, maps and drawings   £12.95

This book chronicles the story of the Home Guard in Worcestershire from its formation in May 1940 to its disbandment in December 1945, as well as its re-creation in the 1950s. It tells of the gradual equipping of the force, its initial and subsequent roles, its increasing professionalism (and associated burgeoning administration), the move from an ethos of volunteering to one of enforced participation backed up by fines for non-attendance, the structure and organization, the characters of some of the officers and men, the establishment of the Auxiliary Units, the increasing role played by women, the training and exercises that its members had to undergo, and of false alarms, incidents and accidents. It is the result of years of work, involving both interviewing former Home Guards and trawling through mounds of Home Guard paperwork, including some records no longer available for inspection.